JUST A THOUGHT SERIES!

BOOK 1

Charles A. Birai; DMIN

Table of Contents

INTRODUCTION

It was in 1973, that I was privileged to buy my own Bible; and with that, began my long journey of daily studying and searching in great humility the sure word of God.

It didn't take me long before I realized that to understand and appreciate the word of God, I needed the Holy Spirit to inspire and help me to understand and interpret the Scriptures. Further, I realized that faith in the living God, and daily earnest prayer before studying the word of God and having an open-mindedness were but a must do. The following Scriptures became very paramount and opened my eyes to see that which the Lord God wanted me to see.

"If any of you lacks wisdom, you should ask God, who gives generously to all without finding fault, and it will be given to you." (James 1:5)

"And without faith, it is impossible to please God, because anyone who comes to him must believe that he exists and that he rewards those who earnestly seek him." (Hebrews 11:6)

"You study the Scriptures diligently because you think that in them you have eternal life. These are the very Scriptures that testify about me.' (John 5:39)

"Thy word is a lamp unto my feet, and a light unto my path." (Psalms 119:105)

I was particularly intrigued by the gospels (Matthew, Mark, Luke, and John). I was mesmerized by the way Jesus took the very ordinary to explain the deeper spiritual lessons. The more I read the gospels and the entire Bible, the more I longed and earnestly prayed for wisdom that comes from above to help me do the same. I wanted to be able to connect the daily happenings with spiritual lessons.

Later, I was introduced to the writings of Ellen G White, my favorite author that knocked down my ego, changed my attitude towards the things of God, made me a humble seeker of the truth, and increased my faith. The more I read, the more I felt inspired or compelled to share with others that which I had read in great humility and accepted by faith without any questions whatsoever.

I, therefore, started writing daily "just a thought" devotions, articles if you wish, and sent them out to church members, friends, the community, public forums and anywhere, where I would find receptive hearts. I was writing so many of these thoughts that someone suggested that I start my own blog whereby I would post these thoughts to whoever wanted instead of filling people's boxes with as many as 5-7 thoughts a day. It was that suggestion that gave birth to: www.pastorbirai.com. This blog was set in such a way that I could post an article at any time. Readers in return would read and comment. The blog became so popular as it attracted new subscribers on a daily basis.. Given that anything unfortunate would happen to the blog thus leading to losing the articles, others suggested that I write a book on the same. That way, many would benefit.

This book, "*Just a thought series, book 1*" is the first of the thoughts randomly selected. In it, you will find thoughts that have inspired some and challenged others to re-examine their way of seeing/viewing things. I hope and pray that by reading, you will be able to appreciate the things of God and live to serve Him and His children while you are still around.

Some Feedback/Reflections by Some Readers/Subscribers

From the time I started writing and posting "Just a thought" write-ups some wrote to share what it meant to them. Here below, please find some of them:

"Great site! I like the way you explain everything without using complicated terms."

- (Anonymous)

Pr. Birai,
"I have always valued your messages daily and I pray that God will continually bless you in all ways."

- (Zach Atinda)

"Wow! This was a real quality post. In theory, I'd like to write like this too - taking time and real effort to make a good article... but what can I say... I keep putting it off and never seem to get something done."

- (Magnetic sponsoring)

"I read your post and I found it amazing. Your thought process is wonderful. The way you express yourself is awesome. Hey, your blog is great. I will bookmark it and I plan to visit regularly."

- (Distance learning)

"This is a really good post. Must admit that you are amongst the best bloggers I have read. Thanks for posting this informative article."

- (Anonymous)

"This is a really good post. Must admit that you are amongst the best bloggers I have read. Here are lots of great information and inspiration, both of which we all need."

- (Cabo San Lucas)

"Excellent read, I just passed this on to a colleague who was doing a little research on this topic."

- (Anonymous)

"Amen Pastor! These devotional passages are so treasurable. My devotion time now starts when I see your 1st message light. We praise God!"

- (Sister Ruth)

"I really enjoyed this post. You describe this topic very well. I enjoy reading your blog and I will definitely bookmark it! Keep up the interesting posts!"

- (Oslo)

"Congratulations Pastor Birai on your 30th Wedding Anniversary. I pray that God may continue to bless you with Good health, Wisdom so that you can continue ministering to us. Reading from you every day is such an inspiration. Congratulations to your wife too for going through this journey with you."

- (Olivia)

"This is a really good post. Must admit that you are amongst the best bloggers I have read. Thanks for posting this informative article."

- (Designer Sarees)

"You made some good points there. I searched for the topic and found most people will agree with your blog. Thanks."

- (All the way from Canada)

"I was very pleased to find this site. I wanted to thank you for this great read!! I definitely enjoyed every little bit of it, and I have you bookmarked to check out the new stuff you post."

- (Buy medicines online)

"I read your post and I found it amazing. Your thought process is wonderful. The way you express yourself is awesome. Hey, your blog is great. I will bookmark it and I plan to visit regularly."

- (Online pharmacy prescription)

"I like this concept. I visited your blog for the first time and have just been your fan. Keep posting as I am going to come to read it every day!"

- (Online Trading)

"This is such a great resource that you are providing, and you give it away for free."

- (Anonymous)

"I wanted to thank you for this great read!! I definitely enjoy every little bit of it I have you bookmarked to check out new stuff you post."

- (Hotel Management Institute)

Pastor Birai, greetings.
This is just to congratulate you for Godly messages that you often send, they remind me of many good things that no one

else ordinarily does. Who knows! You may save many who read them though have not appreciated. Stay blessed and keep it up.

- (Ignatius)

As a college student, I can say that I have personal experience with these things. Growing up in a family of alcoholics I took part in the drinking of alcohol since a very young age. For years I was battling with myself (& the rest of the world) to quit these things. I am now alcohol free. Drinking is a fleshy worldly thing. It is both a disease and a lifestyle; but even above that, alcoholism is an addiction. The act of drinking is a fleshy-worldly, consummative act, which leads one out of the palm of God's hand, into the realms of temptation and sin. Drinking alcohol is done by those who are lost. Lost people are addicted to this drunken state. So, I agree with both #1 and #2, but I believe there is a little more to it than that. Saved people, those who are truly saved (I was just saved this year on Easter, and it took me a little time to realize how Christ is, has, and will save me...) but truly saved people will grow day by day and find themselves not lost in this alcoholism. Those who are truly not saved, you will find them still drinking- unable to let go of the habit/addiction/disease/lifestyle. Alcoholism is a disease. Dis-ease of oneself. Someone uncomfortable or not in truth/touch with oneself will take part in this alcoholism/drunken state out of lost disparity.

- (Katie Mae)

Thanks for a very interesting post. I have high regard for the valuable information you offer in your articles. I really believe you will do much better in the future.

- (Exclusively weddings)

"I just wanted to grant you a shout from the valley of the sun, great information. Much appreciated."

- (IT jobs)

"Great work! You gave a nice post to us. Thanks for spending the time to discuss this, I feel strongly about it and love learning more on this topic."

- (Abacus mental arithmetic)

You write so well, what was your diploma title?

- (Research paper)

I am thankful to you for this great read!! You did a very great job, keep it up.

- (Yacht charter Greece)

Pastor Birai
Splendid. This is worth reading especially around Christmas time. It rekindled a recent analysis by Jirus Jagem on the Biblical story of Cain and Abel on one hand and the other between Joseph and his brothers who sold him into slavery in Egypt because of family jealousy and rivalry.
The cracks of your discourse which is educative and as I can unmask it is that; we should not see things at face value for among us, indeed sometimes those close to us mostly harbor are ill motive. Some are genuinely kind and loving to us. I recall reading a book while in secondary school many years ago

entitled, 'An enemy from within', I am not sure if the author is Okot'b' tek or what was the name, or it is someone else. Otherwise, MERRY XMAS & HAPPY START TO 2011.

- (Joram)

Pastor Birai,
Thank you so much for your articles, they have been a blessing to me during the years, when is the book with the articles coming out? I just found out 'thing I have never found or known about the friendship of David & Jonathan. Merry Christmas and God bless!!

- (Hamabwe)

"Really a beautiful synopsis of the way God asks us to live! Have a blessed Christmas!"

- (Marilyn)

Dear Absalom, That is beautiful!

- (Ed)

Wow. This is deep and personal. Thank you for sharing this. May the Lord bless you as you touch lives in your ministry?

- (Dr. J. W)

DEDICATION

With great joy and satisfaction, I dedicate this book to the following:

To my dear wife, Rachel, for daily reminding me that I have a unique talent for putting thoughts together.

To our loving children-Mary, Daniel, Thomas, and Mary Anne for reading my thoughts then and complaining that they were just too many. Their complaints gave me a sense of what others felt and challenged me to learn to write less

To my former president, Elder Ed Barnett, President, Minnesota conference of SDA, Minnesota, USA, for finding time daily, to read some of my thoughts and always encouraging me to write a book.

To all those who took time to read my thoughts, then and wrote to state of how a particular article blessed them.

It's my hope and prayer that this book will speak to your heart and inspire you to not only share but also go out every single day with the intention to touch /inspire/bless/lighten someone.

FOREWORD

Pastor Absalom Birai has been a friend and fellow pastor for many years. He has a close walk with God, and I have often been encouraged as I have seen God lead in Pastor Absalom's life. He started writing stories that told of God's leading and I am so happy that at last, he has decided to put these stories into book form. I am sure that as you read through this book you will see how God has led in Pastor Absalom's life

The stories are everyday events showing and demonstrating the power of God working in the lives of His people here on earth. As you read, you can't help but realize that God can work in your life in the same way as He has worked in Pastor Absalom's

Enjoy living in the Lord, your life will be blessed!

- Ed Barnett, immediate former President of Rocky Mountain conference. Jan 5th, 2022.

I Need Someone to Host My Guest

I have an urgent request to make to anyone who won't mind helping! I just received word that my friend, will be in your neighborhood for the next several days! Since I will not be there to receive and accommodate Him, I thought I should make an appeal to all my friends to see if anyone will be willing to accommodate Him. I know for a fact that everyone is busy. However, if anyone can sacrifice and do it, please let me know to pass over the information! Please know and understand that I am willing and more than happy to meet all the expenses! Act today, please! So that it can help you to prepare, please note the following about my guest:

1. He is known to wake up very early in the morning to pray (Mark 1:35). Kindly do not disturb Him.
2. As it's His custom, He attends church every 7th day of the week (Luke 4:16). He never misses going to church and He is always on time.
3. He is so humble that He can sleep on the floor without ever complaining. All He sees in your home; He will leave it there. (Philippians 2:5-8)
4. His hobbies include preaching, teaching, and healing all kinds of diseases. (Matthew 4;23)
5. He is a good friend of children. He treats them with dignity and as candidates of the heavenly kingdom (Matthew 19:13-14).
6. He does not practice or even tolerates partiality or favoritism whatsoever. Make sure that you don't gossip. He likes everybody and never speaks ill of anybody.
7. If you can set some time aside, please give Him a tour of your neighborhood. As you go around with Him, please

know that He is known to attract a large crowd of people and that He is ever ready to answer any question from anybody.

8. He spends most of His time thinking of ways to end His Father's work on earth. He gets so much involved to the extent that He has no time to eat.
9. I hope that you will remember to pray before you eat, go to bed, and whenever you wake up in the morning.
10. Please know that He goes by so many names and therefore needs to be careful how you introduce Him. Some of His names/titles include Man of Galilee, Prince of Peace Son of David, Comforter, Counselor, Immanuel, Jesus, the Word, Lord of Lords, King of Kings, I am, and Alpha and Omega.

And lastly, please know that He is one friend that you will never regret to have made. As a matter of fact, He will love to be your friend too.

Volunteers for Jesus

I do recall vividly the day mother Teresa died and how the world mourned her passing on! Why? Mother Teresa gave it all to the people she loved with all her heart. Yea, she went out of her way to minister to the untouchables of Calcutta, India. What a ministry!

Many, like her, have always been moved by compassion and a desire to minister unto others on a volunteer basis. Do we have any examples of volunteers out there? Yes indeed. Here below are some:

- Those who compose Christian songs and charge a minimal fee, barely enough to keep their ministry going. The best we can do to such ones is to promote them by buying their music.
- Pastors who minister on a volunteer basis.
- Many Christians who serve at various positions without pay.
- Men and women, young and old who do everything possible to feed the poor, the orphans, and many others.
- Missionaries who over the years have left their comfort zones and travelled to far away countries to minister to God's children
- Those who are unable to travel but always go an extra mile in sending some financial support to organizations that are meetings the needs of others

What about the good Lord? How does He regard such volunteers? I like the way Jesus answered Peter's question! Here's what peter asked,

"We have left everything to follow you! What then will there be for us?" (Mathew 19:27).

How did Jesus answer that question? Jesus said to them, "I tell you the truth, at the renewal of all things, when the Son of Man sits on his glorious throne, you who have followed me will also sit on twelve thrones, judging the twelve tribes of Israel. And everyone who has left houses or brothers or sisters or father or mother or children or fields for my sake will receive a hundred times as much and will inherit eternal life." (Mathew 19:28-29).

To all the Volunteers, I say, press on by faith for the good Lord will grant you success. He did not bring you this far only to abandon you. He will provide each day at a time.

Looked Out

Ever been locked out? Today, I had some church programs that I needed to print at the club house-housing office. I carried the house keys, or so I thought, that I needed for the 2 doors before reaching my apartment, and the clubhouse keys, that I needed to open 2 doors before reaching the printing room. At the clubhouse, I was disappointed to find out that what I had carried were the car keys! Wow! I, therefore, did not have the clubhouse keys and the house keys! What a way to start the day. Thank God that I remembered to carry my cell phone!

When I left the house, it was only my wife who was awake. The rest were deeply a sleep, as it was only 7:00 Am. For some reason, my wife did not pick up the phone and so there I was standing at the door like a criminal wanting to break in. It was at this point that several things ran through my little computer. Here are some of them:

- I remembered those who have locked themselves out of their cars and had to call someone else to come and open. Unfortunately, it often comes with a price to pay.
- I remembered parents who stepped out of a car but accidently locked themselves out with their little children inside the car.
- I remembered motorists who have stopped to use the restroom while traveling from one State to another but unfortunately locked themselves out of their cars.
- I remembered people who have locked themselves out of their cars and from their houses at the same time!

Does the Bible carry any such stories? You bet!

- Do you recall the story of 10 virgins that went out to meet the bridegroom as found out in Mathew Chapter 25? 5 of them, the foolish ones, were locked out due to their carelessness that led to a lack of thorough preparation.
- How about the story of a man without the wedding garment as told again by Jesus? He was cast and locked outside the wedding banquet.

Listen, It pains me to realize that when the son of man finally returns, many will sadly be locked out from the kingdom! So, what's the solution? The solution is found in Revelation 3: 20, whereby Jesus presents Himself as standing at the doors of our hearts wanting to come in. Will you let Him in?

In Our Journey Home

From that fateful day when Adam and Eve fell from grace and sadly brought about the sufferings that we continue to experience/witness daily, many have made attempts to connect with the Lord of the universe!

As it were, with the eyes fixed on the New Jerusalem, the home of the saints, many have entered the race of traveling home at different times. Unfortunately, some have fallen by the wayside.

If there is but one clear message that has been repeated from the book of Genesis to Revelation, is that for anyone to succeed in this journey, he or she must, and I repeat, must go by "thus said the Lord".

It's therefore important for all the travelers to spend more time reading, understanding, and applying God's requirements as outlined in His Holy manual-the Bible. Any other attempt will not and cannot work!

As you travel, I would like you to remember the following facts/principles:

1. The devil will use his many agents to try to discourage you. Be wary of his many traps
2. You must fix your eyes upon Jesus, who alone can shield, protect, and see you through. Your motto must be "forward ever and backward never"
3. Remember that there is no situation that is permanent in this world. Whatever the roadblocks, Jesus will see you through.

4. As the word of God tells us, whoever endures to the end, the same shall be saved. (Mathew24:13)

Even so, help us dear God to go by your precepts and not man's traditions, opinion, reasoning, and deceptions.

Children and the Fifth Commandment

It's one of those stories that stuck into my memory and pop up every time I need it. The Pastor had just completed delivering a very powerful sermon on the home of the saints and how the saints will always enjoy and appreciate being with their God. As he was about to sit down, a little boy at the back of the Sanctuary raised his hand wanting to ask a question. "Pastor, did you say that all Christians will go to heaven?" asked the little boy, to the amazement of the entire congregation." Yes sir," answered the preacher. "Will my mother go?" asked the little boy. "I believe so," answered the preacher. "If my mother goes, I will not go" answered the little boy."

It so happened that the mother who was a loving and very dedicated leader of the church was something else at home. Sounds familiar?

What am I trying to say? The 5th commandment states, "Honor your father and your mother that your days may be long upon the land which the Lord your God gives you" (Exodus 20:12). The apostle Paul writing to the Ephesians (Ephesians 6; 1-3), repeated the same but added something else, "And you fathers, do not provoke your children to wrath but bring them up in the nurture and admonition of the Lord" (Ephesians 6:4). Those of us who have children, can understand when I say that rearing children have never been all that easy. While it's true that some parents haven't done as much to raise their children in a Christian way, one can also state that no matter how you raise them, some are likely to disappoint you in one way or the other.

Should children obey their parents? There is no question about that. The Bible states that and we must teach it. But remember that the enemy is also at work 24x7 and therefore we must cry daily without ceasing. It's very easy to blame our children, but what many parents fail to understand is that they too are to blame. Allow me to point out a few facts/observations:

Some of us teach our children to do things that we don't do. We ask them to read the Bible, go to church, be good to others and many others but then turn around and do the opposite.

1. We drink, smoke, steal, gossip, hate, despise others, but teach them not to behave like us. Such kind of teaching does not work at all.
2. Some of us are worse than dictators. We tend to think that children are there to be seen and not heard. We yell at them, call them names, and threaten to curse them if they don't obey us.
3. Some of us without knowing teach our children to disobey God. We discourage them from going to church or read the Bible
4. Many of us see our grown-up children as babies. We hardly reach a point where we can trust them to make their own choices.

So, do we know or understand what's happening in every home? I am sorry but no. Other than what we read and hear, we have no idea whatsoever as to what is going on. Remember that there are always two sides to every coin. Yes, we should all teach and encourage our children to obey their parents. We should also remind parents to treat their children nicely and stop threatening them with a curse

Keep Your Hands to Yourself

I thank the Creator of the universe for the gift of hands, which help me to write, eat, bath, work, swim, drive, vacuum, greet others, wash dishes, do laundry, and many other things.

That said, it needs to be said and emphasized that these hands have gotten some of us into very serious trouble. By misusing our hands, some of us have gotten into trouble with others and the law. Misuse our hands? How do you mean? Here, look at the following:

1. Some misuse their hands by hitting, slapping, knocking, or fighting someone/others.
2. Some misuse their hands by pulling the trigger and sadly taking another person's life.
3. Some misuse their hands by stealing and carrying things that they know very well to belong to someone else.
4. Some misuse their hands by touching people that they are not supposed to touch. They end up being accused or sued for sexual harassment.

It will help if we use our hands for doing the right or accepted things. As Jesus said, let us do our best to control ourselves or in this case, keep our hands to ourselves. Note the language (figure of speech) that He used:

> *"And if your right hand causes you to sin, cut it off and throw it away. It is better for you to lose one part of your body than for your whole body to go into hell." (Mathew 5:30).*

The emphasis here is self-control rather than literally cutting off our sinful hands. Heavenly Father, we thank you and truly appreciate the gift of hands. But these hands have gotten some of us into trouble. Now we beseech you to help us keep our hands to ourselves. Begin with me, please.

Questioning Our Faith/Beliefs

Out there, are some people who believe in God and are associated with a certain church/ministry/denomination/religion. To some, it was the religion/church of their parents and therefore have always believed that way. To others, they picked it up while in high school or college. And yet to some more others, they were influenced by either their friends or spouses. While it's not up to us to judge as to who is who, at least we can agree on the following:

1. Each believes that his/her religion/church/denomination is the right one.
2. Some believe that God is not all that particular with what day/church/denomination one goes to church or belongs to.
3. Some get really offended if anyone questions or says something about their beliefs/religion/denomination/church.

But since all of us desire to do the right thing and are on a journey with hopes of not only reaching there but also belonging there, it makes sense to approach this issue with a different mindset. How do you mean?

1. We should continue to pray, search and study the Bible daily.
2. We should be open minded and humble to accept areas where we are wrong. No one is always right in every situation.
3. We should be brave enough to make any changes if convicted to do so.
4. We must be willing to question our faith, and if possible, our beliefs.

But why should we take the pain to do all that?

You and I know through experience that we can honestly be wrong. If I say we were taught that 2+2=5 and we have believed that all our life that will not make it right.

1. We should not be like primary school kids who will never accept anything different from what their teacher told them.
2. Some scriptures state very clearly that God indeed cares for some of those things that many of us regard as minute or non-consequential.
3. The Bible states very clearly that some of the faithful ones will be denied entry into the kingdom simply because all they did was listen to the wrong advice.

If you have time, please, pray, read, and reflect on the following:

"Not everyone who says to me, 'Lord, Lord,' will enter the kingdom of heaven, but only he who does the will of my Father who is in heaven. Many will say to me on that day, 'Lord, Lord, did we not prophesy in your name and your name drive out demons and perform many miracles?' Then I will tell them plainly, 'I never knew you; away from me, you evildoers!' (Mathew7:21-23).

"Then Jesus went through the towns and villages, teaching as he made his way to Jerusalem. Someone asked him, "Lord, are only a few people going to be saved?" He said to them, "Make every effort to enter through the narrow door, because many, I tell you, will try to enter and will not be able to. Once the owner of the house gets up and closes the

door, you will stand outside knocking and pleading, 'Sir, open the door for us.'

"But he will answer, 'I don't know you or where you come from.'" Then you will say, 'we ate and drank with you, and you taught in our streets.'" But he will reply, 'I don't know you or where you come from; away from me, all you evildoers! '"There will be weeping there, and gnashing of teeth, when you see Abraham, Isaac and Jacob and all the prophets in the kingdom of God, but you yourselves thrown out. People will come from east and west and north and south and will take their places at the feast in the kingdom of God. Indeed, there are those who are last who will be first, and first who will be last."(Luke 13:22-30)

Does the Bible support this way of thinking? Yes indeed, it does, "Test everything. Hold on to the good" (1 Thessalonians 5:21)

All I am saying is that let us put everything on the table and do a thorough examination. It will be good for our salvation.

Living With a Complicated Spouse

There are spouses who are just too complicated to live with. What's wrong with them?

1. They are hard to understand and deal with.
2. They are troublemakers, whiners, irritating, and have majored in cursing, quarreling, and complaining all the time for who knows what.
3. They are nothing but dictators in their own homes. It's either their way of doing things or nothing else passes. They have thirsty for power and control.
4. They are good out there but something else in their own homes.
5. They are liars, loves to argue and take pleasure to subject their family to uncalled for headache.

In trying to deal with their complicated partners, some have found relief in the book of Proverbs. Why proverbs? Because in a way some have misunderstood it to mean that they are allowed to walk away from their quarrelsome spouses. Even though Solomon addressed some of the statements to women, the truth of the matter is that there are men who are worse than women in many ways of life. Read on:

"Better to live on a corner of the roof than sharing a house with a quarrelsome wife."(Proverbs 21:9)

"A quarrelsome wife is as annoying as constant dripping on a rainy day."(Proverb 27:15)

"Better to live in a desert than with a quarrelsome and ill-tempered wife." (Proverbs21:19)

So what is the way out? Allow me to suggest the following:

1. 1. Plead with the good Lord to help your spouse change.
2. 2. Let your spouse know how you feel and how what he or she does makes things worse
3. 3. Purpose in your heart to try and let go of those things that you do and say that annoys your spouse.
4. 4. Practice forgiveness, tolerance, and just ignore certain things.
5. 5. Do everything possible to find time to read the Bible together, pray together, and go to church together.

Lessons Learned From the Chile Mine Rescue

September/October 2010 will be remembered for among other things the months when, the world found itself thinking, sympathizing, and praying for 33 miners trapped underneath the land-half a mile down the earth. If anything, this incident has reminded us of how powerless we're and that whether we like it or not, there come moments in our lives whereby we'll be forced to seek God's intervention.
Much as the miners and their families looked unto their Government to help them, one can conclude that their highest comfort was in the living God. One miner said it all, when he pointed out that underneath their prison, there was God and the devil. He chose to cling to God who indeed did not disappoint them! What a moving testimony!.

It goes without saying that many of us for reasons best known to us, try to isolate God from our daily lives. When everything seems to be going right, we divorce God from our system and treat Him like He doesn't matter!

Here is the truth of the matter. There comes a time in our lives when we are willing to give up everything just so that we can be alive. Unfortunately, it so happens that by then, no one needs that which you are offering.

The stories and pictures from Chile have truly touched and humbled me in ways I cannot explain. I sincerely thank the good Lord for yet another miracle before the entire world. God has reminded us once again that He and not us is in charge.

Let us all purpose in our hearts to seek God now when He can be found. A time comes when God will declare" It's finished." Well, can anyone doubt or question the fact that not that many of us want to die?

Even so dear Lord, teach us humility and remind each one of us that we are nothing without you. Amen

Not Fair At All

When it comes to fairness, many of us lack it big time. Fairness embraces the golden rule as taught by our Lord and Savior Jesus Christ:" So in everything, do to others what you would have them do to you, for this sum up the Law and the Prophets." (Mathew7:12) But what does this mean? Allow me to use some illustrations:

1. Do to your family members (spouse, children, parents, siblings, and relatives) only those things that you would like to be done unto you.
2. If you don't want anyone to mislead your spouse or children, then you must not even contemplate it.
3. The way you talk to others must be the same way you would like others to talk to you.
4. If you don't like people talking behind your back, you also should stop talking about others
   5. If you don't like people criticizing you just for the fun of it, then you must not make criticizing others your toy.
5. 6. Wherever you are and whatever you are doing, behave and treat others the same way that you would like to be treated.
6. 7. We must all be as good leaders as we are followers.
7. 8. If you want people to appreciate you, then you also must learn to appreciate others.
8. 9. If you don't want people to take advantage of you, then you must stop taking advantage of others.
9. 10. If you don't like people who cheat you, then you must quit cheating others yourself.

Bottom line. Let us be fair to all God's children.

Lord Jesus, please teach us how to be fair in all our daily dealings with all your children. Help us to remember that charity begins at home. Help us to let arrogance and stubbornness go and instead plant humility and the concept of fairness in our hearts. Begin with me, please.

The Why Me Question

Occasionally, tragedy decides to visit us, not just once, but several times, thus leaving one devastated beyond human explanation. Whenever that happens, almost all find themselves asking this painful question "Why me?"

While I don't think that any human being can give a satisfactory answer to such a question, allow me to address this issue from a different perspective. Any time tragedy strikes, there are in my opinion at least three ways of looking at it:

1. Firstly, it's possible that such a tragedy came as a result of one's unwise decision. Many are the people who have dug their own graves and buried themselves. Some chose to do certain things that they know very well will lead to tragedy. Like what? Like stealing, abusing drugs, drinking, and driving under the influence of alcohol, hanging out at the wrong places, at the wrong time, and with the wrong people.
2. Secondly, such would be the work of the enemy. The words of Peter say it all," Be self-controlled and alert. Your enemy the devil prowls around like a roaring lion looking for someone to devour" (1 Peter 5:8). When on earth, Jesus warned repeatedly about the enemy and his many snares. I will cite some of the warnings:

"The owner's servants came to him and said, 'Sir, didn't you sow good seed in your field? Where then did the weeds come from? 'An enemy did this,' he replied. (Mathew 13:27-28)

"Simon, Simon, Satan has asked to sift you as wheat. But I have prayed for you, Simon that your faith may not fail. And

when you have turned back, strengthen your brothers." (Luke 22:31-32)

3. Thirdly, it's possible that the Lord allowed such tragedy to accomplish His will in our lives. How so? If you can, reflect on the following:
   - Do you remember the story of Job? It was all of God's doing.
   - Do you recall the story of the children of Israel? God sent them into captivity for 70 years.
   - Do you recall John the Baptist? Jesus was able to save him but instead, let him die in prison. Why in the world did He do that? To become a source of encouragement to millions of those who will be called to go through such an ordeal.
   - Whether we get all these or not, we need to form a good relationship with our God such that when bad things happen to us, we can say this:

"Though he slays me, yet will I trust in him" (Job 13:15)

"And we know that in all things God works for the good of those who love him, who have been called according to his purpose" (Romans 8:28)

The rest, we can leave with our God who only knows the end from the beginning. Yes, in the world, we shall suffer persecution but let us always remember that He will never leave or forsake us no matter what. Therefore, cheers fellow travelers. Soon, we'll be home where tragedy will be the thing of the past.

Ten Lepers: Which One Tells Your Story?

During the time of Jesus on earth, leprosy was a very dreadful disease. Once you came down with it, you were isolated from your family, community or even attending the synagogue. As if that was not enough pain, one was supposed to go round ringing a bell and shouting "unclean." Jesus told a story of 10 lepers that He healed. Out of the 10, only one returned to thank Him. Read the story and note how Jesus reacted:

> *"Now on his way to Jerusalem, Jesus traveled along the border between Samaria and Galilee. As he was going into a village, ten men who had leprosy met him. They stood at a distance and called out in a loud voice, "Jesus, Master, have pity on us!" When he saw them, he said, "Go, and show you to the priests." And as they went, they were cleansed. One of them, when he saw he was healed, came back, praising God in a loud voice. He threw himself at Jesus' feet and thanked him—and he was a Samaritan. Jesus asked, "Were not all ten cleansed? Where are the other nine? Was no one found to return and give praise to God except this foreigner?" Then he said to him, "Rise and go; your faith has made you well."(Luke 17:11-19)*

In your lifetime, the good Lord has blessed you in more ways than one. You can bear testimony of that; repeatedly, he has not only forgiven you but picked you up from the ashes and provided you with not one but all your needs. But how do you evaluate yourself? What is it that you have done for Him?

When do you think of the 10 lepers, which one tells your story?

God, please have mercy on us; for we always think more about ourselves and very little, if anything about you. Indeed, we are selfish people. I am chief among them. Forgive, I pray. Amen.

Minutes Away From My Destination

If I'm finally lost, it will not be because the good Lord did not do enough to warn me, but rather due to my total failure to learn from the many daily warnings! Indeed, the good. Lord continues to speak to my heart daily. Today was yet another very strong message.

Today, I left home at 4:45 pm for the post office that is only 10-minute drive away. I knew that I had enough time to make it to the post office! What I did not anticipate was a traffic jam! And to my great disappointment, there was an accident that involved three cars, and as you can imagine, traffic was so slow. By the time I arrived at the post office, I was 2 minutes late! Wow! It was on my way home when it hit me hard! Just think about the following facts:

1. I made a fool of myself by thinking that I had plenty of time! Don't we all do this even in matters as important as our salvation!
2. All it took to miss entry to the post office was a mere 2 minutes late. Many of us cheat ourselves by comforting ourselves that we have taken care of the major issues of sin. Often, what we forget is that it's the "small sins" (gossip, hatred, little cheating, rudeness, arrogance, jealousy, and many others that count). Many of us will be shocked at the last minute when God himself will solemnly declare "Sorry son/daughter! I can't find your name!" What a sad day will that be!

The good news is I will make another attempt tomorrow! The sad news as regards our salvation is that when Jesus finally gets here, there will be no more tomorrow! Then, you will realize that it's too late to do anything! What will you say or do then! I guess nothing really!

But I have good news for you today. There is still time. The question is:" Will I wake up from my slumber and do the right thing now?

An Evil Report

From the time the promise was given to the Patriarch Abram to its fulfillment, a lot of water had gone under the bridge. As you follow what turned out to be the most painful journey, you can't help but wonder if ever, God's children ever learned any lesson. Come with me as together we tip toe the painful history of God's elect. Time and space will only allow for the highlights:

1. Abram and Sarah doubted God's promises, took matters into their own hands, and did that which caused them more pain.
2. The young man Joseph was sold by his own blood brothers in an attempt to hinder him from being their leader.
3. Joseph became the prime minister in a foreign land by God's providence. He became a savior to his family after many years of suffering
4. Egypt was destroyed by the merciful God when Pharaoh stood on His way to liberate His children
5. The journey that was supposed to have taken them just one week took them 40 years in the wilderness
6. Of the 647,000 people, besides women and children who left Egypt to the Promised Land, only two made it, Joshua and Caleb. The rest were destroyed in the wilderness for what the Bible describes as "the hardness of their hearts." They complained, whined, and tested God to the uttermost. Some were swallowed by the opening of the land due to challenging God's choice of Moses, as their leader. Even Moses, the meekest man on earth did not make it to the Promised Land.

7. When they had come to the borders of the Promised Land, God instructed Joshua to send 12 men to go and spy the land. These were good and able leaders. On their return, 10 of them rendered what the Bible terms "an evil report," that caused a lot of pain and commotion in the camp. Thank God for Joshua and Caleb, who stood tall and told nothing but the whole truth. Their resolve saved a situation that would have turned chaotic. That it's only these two who made it to the Promised Land underscores the fact that God is mindful of those things that more often than not we regard as minute.

Many years after the story took place and of course, recorded for our own benefit, the big question still remains, has anyone learned a lesson, any lesson! Have I? Have You? What is very clear from the story is this: Although God in many times acts like He doesn't care about what goes on in any country or community, there comes a time when He intervenes and acts in a way that leaves no doubts in many peoples' minds that He is unhappy. You and I need to tread very carefully when it comes to dealing with God. The classic warning "Do not be deceived: God cannot be mocked. A man reaps what he shows." (Galatians 6:7," remains true today. Tread carefully, I repeat. Will you?

A Woman Who Would Not Give Up

The story of the Canaanite woman as found in Mathew 15:21-28 goes to prove that nothing can stop those who love their Lord from either following Him or serving Him.

Although not a Jew, she had this very strong faith that Jesus Christ of Nazareth was more than able to heal her daughter who had suffered for a long time. That is why she came crying "Have mercy on me, O Lord, thou son of David; my daughter is grievously vexed with a devil." (Matthew 15:22."

From the time she requested to the time her request was answered, several very disappointing happenings took place that would have easily driven her away. Reflect on the following:

1. Jesus at first ignored her by saying nothing-verse 22
2. The disciples requested Jesus to send her away-verse 22
3. Jesus made it clear that His mission was to seek and find His own people-the Jews/sons and daughters of Abraham-verse 22
4. Despite their negative attitude towards her and their apparent unwillingness to help her, she did that which a nominal follower of Jesus would not have done. Listen to what Matthew says, "Then came she and worshiped him, saying, Lord, help me-verse 25
5. To add insult to injury, Jesus made a very annoying statement. He said "It is not right to take the children's bread and toss it to their dogs." verse 26.

Indeed, many would have left at this point and never t come back. They would have gone round telling others that Jesus called her a dog. That would have developed a grudge towards Jesus and His disciples. In our age and time, they would have either left the church without telling the leaders their reason, but not so with the Canaanite woman. Instead of being offended, she pleaded, "Yes, Lord, "but even the dogs eat the crumbs that fall from their masters 'table." verse 27. Wow! What faith and determination!

What she told Jesus was that she was willing to take the left overs.

She didn't care what Jesus called her and how the disciples treated her. All she ever wanted was to have her daughter healed! Anything else came secondary! That is the kind of faith that works.

At the end of this episode, her request was not only granted but Jesus highlighted her faith. He said "Woman, you have great faith! Your request is granted." And her daughter was healed from that very hour. Hallelujah! Praise be unto the name of the living God!

Ever been disappointed and felt like either moving to another church or doing away with your faith altogether! I appeal you to read this story again! At the end of the story ask yourself this thought-provoking question. Placed in the position of the Canaanite woman, would you have quit or continued begging for help! Will you!

They Chose To Stay With Jesus

Even after we have accepted the good Lord into our lives, the devil works overtime in trying to win us back into his camp. Unfortunately, many of us have fallen victim to take note of Peter's admonition: "Be self-controlled and alert. Your enemy the devil prowls around like a roaring lion looking for someone to devour." 1 Peter 5:8. How has he succeeded? Below are some examples:

1. He has convinced several to be unfaithful in returning to the Lord that which belongs to Him. We are not only good at taking care of our interests but also by defending our status quo of unfaithfulness.
2. He has won in convincing some of us that a day of worship is not a big deal. Even those who know best treat the Sabbath as any other day.
3. Some are leaving church every single week because some preachers preached or said something unpleasing to them.

Does this mean that all have fallen, victims? By no means! Over the years, there are those who have stood firm against all odds.

Have you ever been misunderstood! It may come as a surprise to some of us to note that Jesus was misunderstood all the time. In John chapter 6, he gave a discourse on the eating of his body and drinking of His blood that led to many forsaking him. Let us have John describe the reaction. He writes: "On hearing it, many of his disciples said "This is a hard teaching. Who can accept it? From this time many of his disciples turned back and no longer followed him." (John 6:60; 66.).

How about His disciples? Let us have Peter answer that question.

> *"You do not want to leave too, do you?" Jesus asked the Twelve. Simon Peter answered him, "Lord, to whom we shall go? You have the words of eternal life. We believe and know that you are the Holy One of God." (John 6:67-68."*

If you were there, would you have left or stayed?

Another Disappointment

Has anyone ever disappointed you? How did you feel? Well, I have been through this disappointment thing several times already. Every time I think that I have mastered the art and science of disappointment, Lo and behold, another one pops up, sometimes with devastating effects.

See, over the years, many have let me down. Included in the list but not limited have been,

1. Those that I considered and treated as my intimate friends. They let me down or betrayed me at the point when I really needed them, thus tempting me to question the rationale behind their friendship.
2. Leaders that I knew or so I thought that they were going to make great changes for the benefit of God's children. However, as soon as they ascended into power, they forgot where they had come from thus making life for their subjects even worse than before
3. People that I greatly contributed to their success in life. After they achieved their goal, they dropped me and picked up new friends. The only time I have seen them come back was when they needed more help.

Not long ago, I suffered yet another disappointment which sadly reminded me of all the previous ones. The strange thing about this disappointment is that it was not by a fellow human being but strangely by a vacuum cleaner. Let me explain.

Let me confess that I love to vacuum. From the years of my graduate studies when I did custodial work, I hate to see a messy carpet. As you can imagine, I have used all kinds of vacuum cleaners both at my place of work and at my home.

So, I bought this small, but very useful shark vacuum cleaner that I nicknamed "my friend" From the day it made its way to our home, I knew that this type of vacuum cleaner was unique in more ways than one: How so? It was not only lighter than all the others that I had owned but also did not make too much noise.

It had served me very well until one morning when I discovered that what I had thought to be a unique vacuum cleaner was after all the same as all others, if not worse. It died just like that. There were no prior warnings or any other symptoms. It did not even care that the job was halfway done.

Now that I think about it, I blame myself for counting on a vacuum cleaner that was ironically put together by fellow human beings, some of whom have disappointed me over the years.

tin the end, I decided to take care of this disappointment game once and for all by turning up my eyes upon Jesus, who alone has never and will never disappoint me. How about you my friend?

Come and Meet My Doctor

One Tuesday afternoon, I went to see my doctor for or a regular checkup. During the period that I was there, I found myself seriously thinking about the relationship between a patient and his/her personal doctor. A lot of things went through my mind. Here are some reflections:

1. It's the patient who makes the initiative to see the doctor by calling and setting up an appointment.
2. It's up to the patient to divulge the information stating the symptoms-even that cannot be told to the close family members and friends to help the doctor to come up with the right prescription.
3. The medicine prescribed may or may not heal the patient.
4. There are as many doctors as there are lines of a medical career that one has chosen to pursue.
5. Regardless of their line of study, there is one disease that no human being can heal? Really! Which one? It's the sin disease.

And that is why I wish to appeal to whoever is willing, to come and meet my Doctor-Jesus of Nazareth, the poor man from Galilee. He alone is known to have healed all manner of disease and sickness. He is such an expert that you don't have to tell Him of your sickness both physical and spiritual. All you need to do is to come and meet Him. His touch alone not only heals but restores one at the same time. What about the fee? It's free!

I say yes to His invitation every single day. Would you like to meet my doctor?

As We Wait For His Second Coming

You and I know from reading the sure word of God that this world will one day come to an end. Equally true, is the fact that some of us might not live to witness that glorious occasion! What has been disturbing to watch is individuals who have confused themselves in their waiting. Do you mean there are such kinds of people? Yes indeed. Here are some of them.

1. In the late '70s, he quit/gave up on almost everything in readiness for His 2nd coming. When things didn't go like they were thinking, they gave up their faith.
2. As the year 2000 approached, many became so worried about His soon return that they decided to get ready! Since many of them were moved by fear, when the time passed by, they too abandoned their faith.
3. How about now? The financial turmoil in the world has let some declare that this is it. As always, some have gone around preaching and encouraging others to sell their homes because the end of the world has come! I have even heard cases of students who arc trying to drop out of school because Jesus is coming.

And so how do we go about it! Here is what I have learned in great humility!

1. We must learn never go to ahead of God. Let us not try to force God to return.
2. God will sure return, but on His timetable, and not ours.
3. The news of His coming should bring gladness to our hearts and not fear and panic.
4. A daily and thorough preparation is needed to avoid a last-minute over-reaction. We need a daily and true connection with our Lord.

5. Avoid the temptation of extremes. Many have been misled and frustrated in the end.
6. Remember that the devil is working hard-24X7-to deceive, if possible, even the very elect.
7. Before you rush into dropping everything to preach, remember that charity begins at home. Therefore, start with yourself first. Once you have worked on yourself, ask the Lord to use you wherever you are.

Let us all use the daily signs in helping us to prepare and not to mislead us and others. "Watch out for the devil," is my sincere appeal to each one of us! Do you see my point!

Daily Decisions

Each day of our lives, we are faced with very difficult/challenging decisions: Like which ones?

1. Decision on whether to be a peacemaker or a troublemaker.
2. Decision on whether to change career or continue with what we have.
3. Decision on whether to do away with a habit that we know very well that with time it will destroy us or continue until we die or are caught.
4. Decision on whether to change our attitude and be kind, gentle, considerate, or continue to annoy and be on other people's nerves.
5. Decision on whether to accept Jesus Christ as our personal Savior or to continue hardening our hearts.
6. Decision on whether we want to accept other people's opinions or treat others like they don't count.
7. Decision on whether to forgive and carry on or to continue to hate until the last minute.
8. Decision on whether to move to another church where our spiritual needs will be made or to remain royal and support our church in all ways.
9. Decision on whether to focus on school and leave other things that might affect us forever or continue to do stuff that you know very well that will hurt both you and those that love and care for you
10. Decision on whether to get married or remain single.

11. Decision on whether to walk away from a marriage relationship or remain faithful to your marriage vows "until death apart us

In any of the above decisions and many others, we'll do well to remember that every decision we make has got its consequences and benefits. Whether we like it or not, we have no choice but to arrive at decision. What you and I must avoid, is to linger between two decisions. So in the end, we must be either hot or cold and not lukewarm.

I will daily consult the Lord Jesus to help me make the right decisions. How about you my friend?

Borrowing a Leaf from the Academic World

Those of us, who have had an opportunity to go to high school/college/university, know that there are chore courses and elective courses that must be done to qualify for graduation! Whereas each student has the freedom to choose any elective, all students for reasons best known to the curriculum designers must take core courses no matter how tough they are! In like manner, in real life, our greatest teacher-Jesus Christ of Nazareth- expects each one of us to enroll for both electives and core courses at His University. Below, are some topics/subjects that may be taken as electives in our daily interaction with others?

- Politics
- Social life
- Business
- Family issues/matters
- Helping others in finding work or going to college
- Entertainment
- Internet chat/correspondence
- Finding a life partner
- Many others like such

The core subjects, in my opinion, should include the following:

- Study of the word of God
- Witnessing
- Research on the last day events

- What the Bible says about many issues that confront us day in, day out.

What has been of great concern everywhere is that most people if not all love to take elective courses and spent all their time there at the expense of the core courses. It seems to me that the core courses herein have been ignored days without number!

Wait a minute! Must all take the core courses? Yes! And here is why! We are only strangers in this world. Today, we are, tomorrow we are gone. And therefore in so many words, God expects all of us to take core courses!

Well, I re-enrolled this morning! How about you!

Dates Worth Remembering

There are certain dates worth remembering; dates that something happened that had an impact on our lives. A failure to remember such dates often time leads to other problems, serious ones at times! Below are some of the dates and the reason why we should remember each one of them!

1. The day you first joined school- Primary/secondary/college?
   - You will appreciate the great sacrifice that was paid by your parents and whoever paid your school fees.
   - You will need to be reminded that the good Lord was there all the way!
2. The first day that you started working?
   - You will appreciate the struggle you went through by attaining the necessary education/training.
   - You will appreciate whoever helped you to get the job.
   - You will realize how lucky you were at the time your friends were still unemployed.
   - You will be reminded that the good Lord was behind every move to help you succeed!
3. The day you said, "I do, till death alone do us part!"
   - You will recall the many sleepless nights as you tried to figure out who it was
   - You will recall all the promises that you uttered from your own mouth and the good plans you had then for your family.

- You will recall how stubborn you were by not listening to anyone who advised you otherwise!
- You will recall the first time your sweetheart came to your home and how excited you were by introducing her/him to everyone. You even carried some of her/his pictures everywhere.
- You will need to be reminded that the good Lord was there through your search and disappointments. In the end, He saw you through

4. The day you migrated to the city/another country!

- You will recall the joy and excitement.
- You will appreciate all those who helped you to settle.
- You will appreciate every contribution that was made by both family and strangers.
- You will be reminded how many hours you spent on your knees pleading with the good Lord to intervene and all the promises that you made to God!

You will be reminded that the good Lord has sure kept all His promises while you have forgotten Him days without number!

5. The day you first believed (For Christ's disciples)

- Will remind you of all the bad things you did before you surrendered.
- Will appreciate the gift of forgiveness and the joy of belonging to God's family.
- Will appreciate those who introduced you to the man of Galilee.

- Will remind you of your promise to leave this world alone and how you have walked away from all your promises.
- Will help you appreciate God's willingness to continually forgive you!

6. How often you have said no to the gentle invitation by the Savior of the world!
   - Will be reminded of how stubborn you have been.
   - Will remind you of the devil's hard work to have you remain in his camp.
   - Will appreciate the prayers of loved ones who would like to see you surrender and lead a better life.
   - Will remind you that everything else was done to save you but you ignored it all

And finally, you and I need to remember that we are but, "a vapor, that appears for a little time, and then vanishes away!" James 4:13

Blessed are those who remember all these things! Are you

The Enemy From Within

Conventional wisdom assumes that when everything else has failed and the enemies from outside are after one's blood, the family members and friends are supposed to stand by and at least give support. But Biblical archives and daily experiences say otherwise!

Throughout the centuries, many have been so hurt and disappointed to know that their downfall or troubles were brought about by those least expected. Look at the following:

1. Genesis 4:8 Tells us that Abel, son of Adam, was killed by his own brother, Cain.
2. Genesis Chapter 37 tells us that Joseph was sold by his own brothers.
3. Our Lord and Savior, Jesus Chris, was opposed by his own brothers, religious leaders, and some of His disciples.
4. In his zeal and passion to plant churches, the apostle Paul became an enemy to many and was opposed and given hard time by those from within.
5. Moses was opposed by his own siblings-Miriam and Aaron

How about our time?

1. Some religious leaders and pastors have been taken aback to know that those behind their sorrows were colleagues.
2. Many Christians have been shocked beyond belief to discover that indeed some of the brothers and sisters in Christ don't like them. Worse still, they wish them evil.

3. Upon promotion, good l luck, or a sign of doing well, many have found themselves facing several challenges only to discover that the one behind all this was one they considered a friend.

The solution to all this is to pay attention to the words of our Lord-Jesus Christ, Said he: "and a man's enemies will be those of his own household." Mathew 10:36

As we go about our daily lives, let us remember that not everyone is happy with us. We should therefore be cautious, talk or share less.

Without A Qualified Advocate/Lawyer

I do recall the day and the hour it happened! I also do recall how I felt and reacted! It was Wednesday, December 10th, 2008, at exactly 3:45 PM, Minnesota time! 15 minutes before I clocked out for the day, one of the supervisors came to my register, turned off the light, and asked me to go and see the assistant manager in his office! Right there, a lot of things went through my mind! Here are some of them!

1. I am fired! Period!
2. I recalled the experience of the previous day. I had been audited and found wanting! I came short of $10.00, because of applying a coupon credit worth that much from another store. Hard to understand how that had happened! But, it happened, and now it seemed as if it had come to haunt me!
3. I did not understand why they wanted to fire me and yet according to me I was doing a good job!
4. I started thinking of the pain and agony of applying for another part-time job and if I would be lucky to get one in this most devastating economic meltdown!

Well, deep in my heart I decided to accept the reality and let things take their own course or better still as the Lord saw fit! Every step, though, towards the assistant manager's office was heavy and full of emotions.

I even decided not to defend myself for any allegations/accusations but rather thank them, lay down the tools, and leave knowing that I had done my best!

"Come in, and have a seat please," said the assistant manager! "Thank you," was my response! Though I seemed composed, deep inside me, I felt a sense of hopelessness, partly because the boss was younger than me by several years!

"How are things?" asked the boss! "Pretty well," was my response as I wondered why he was going around instead of reading my verdict so that I would hit the road returning home with a feeling of a poor performer!

"I called you to let you know what a wonderful job you are doing and the decision to offer you a permanent position," said the assistant manager! It's like I did not hear him correctly! "Everybody is very proud of you and please continue doing a good job," the boss continued! "Do you have any questions for me?" asked the boss! "Not really other than thanking you for the offer!" was my answer. "Well, I must let you go," said the boss! I once again thanked him and left in a hurry lest he changed his mind again!

On my way home, I thought seriously of all that I have heard and learned since becoming a Christian about Judgment! Here is what flashed through my mind:

1. Whether we like it or not, a day is coming when we all will stand before the Lord of the universe to render an account of all that we did while on earth-Ecclesiastes 12:13-14.
2. I felt how powerless/hopeless we'll feel facing the Lord of the universe without the assurance that all our sins had been forgiven and deleted from the records! Worse still, I found myself thinking loud and clear on the feeling of approaching God without a qualified advocate! Then, all our education, status, gender and money will mean nothing!

The good news though is this:

1. There is therefore now no condemnation to them which are in Christ Jesus-Romans 8:1.
2. My little children, these things write I unto you, that ye sin not, And if any man sin, we have an advocate with the Father, Jesus Christ the righteous-I John 2:1

But here is the fact check! Like in any case, you and I must make plans to engage and keep the advocated way before the case comes up! And my question to you and I is this "What's our relationship with the only advocate that will seal our destiny in the fullness of time!

Refused To Be Treated Special

There was a time that God wanted a nation to represent Him to the world. Out of His wisdom, He chose Israel to become that peculiar nation. Israel was supposed to mingle with the world in great humility to pass over the knowledge about the living God. God made it very clear that their success was depended on their obedience to "thus said the Lord."

God kept His promise by blessing them so that their status was better of as compared to all the surrounding nations. Israel conquered all other nations and was greatly feared! Theirs was a rare opportunity that many longed for!

Unfortunately, Israel came to appoint whereby she refused to be called/treated special and instead demanded to be like other nations. Listen to their request:" Now, make us a king to judge us like all other nations." (1 Samuel 8:5.)

When Israel demanded a king to become like other nations, Samuel was displeased as that was but an indication that they had denied God. However, the good Lord went ahead and fulfilled the desires of their hearts. Needless to say, Israel suffered greatly as a result of its actions.

How about our time? It makes my heart sad to note that:

- Out there, there are individuals who have been born into very rich families. However, such, have refused to go to school or hold any kind of job. Their behavior of drinking and breaking the law has been a disgrace to their parents. Once in a while, when some are caught in camera, in the very act of misbehaving, it causes an embarrassment to the concerned families.

- Out there, are individuals, who were born and brought up in Christian homes. Their parents are ministers, church leaders, and what have you. Unfortunately, these individuals abuse drugs, drink like fish, steal, or do all kinds of things, that are a complete betrayal of their family values.
- Out there, are those who have been called by the name of God either as ministers, church officers, or Christians? Instead of being a light unto the world, they are a daily stumbling block.

If you can, take a few moments and reflect on yourself as a person. In view of who you are, where you were born, what position you hold, and many others, have you lived according to your calling, family status, or have you refused to be treated/regarded as special and instead become a complete nuisance?

Deceived By the Clock

Like all other Fridays, this last one was packed with plenty of" to-do stuff!" The day was supposed to start as early as 5:00 AM. Every single item on the list was not only important but had to be done on time otherwise others and I would be affected!

I woke up as early as 4:00 AM, or so I thought! My bathroom clock that had not heretofore let me down, told me that it was 4:40 AM. Knowing that I had plenty of time, I took my time preparing. By the time I made my way to the living room to:

- Do my devotion
- Check and respond to some e-mails
- Make the church program,
- Eat
- Leave to pick a church member from work @ 6:00 AM
- Drop a church member's baby at a babysitter @ 7:00 AM
- Drop her at work by 7:30 AM
- Leave for work at 8:30, I would not believe what I saw!

The living room clock read 6:30 AM. What? Am I dreaming? I asked myself as I stood there speechless! Hard to believe that I had been deceived by the clock! God have mercy! Mad with the clock and myself, I left without doing my devotion, making the church program, checking my e-mails or eating!

Ever been deceived by your clock/watch? What was your reaction? Any lessons learned?

The Life of a Squirrel

If any animals are lucky to be alive, then they must be squirrels. Every single day, I have witnessed some of them narrowly and miraculously missing death by inches. I used to live at this place that ion all accounts looked like a home for squirrels. So, every time I was out there for a walk or drove around, guess what I saw? Squirrels everywhere; closing the road, chasing each other, or climbing the trees.

These little creatures risk their lives by crossing busy roads. There are times that I have found myself closing my eyes or screaming at them to be careful. Not willing to kill them some motorists slow down or stop while others make it by God's grace. Whether these squirrels are able to think and make wise decisions, I do not know. What I do know is that many of us ought to know better and yet every single day, we go about doing certain things that endanger our precious lives. How do you mean?

1. Some indulge in drinking alcohol that has been a killer drink. Many are they who have fallen victims to alcoholic drinks. Many have lost their jobs and families, quit school, and had many other unfortunate situations.
2. Some have chosen to abuse drugs that has have had a lasting impact on their lives and are a concern to those who love and care for them.

3. Some of us are not careful as regards what we consume. We eat anything, all the time, and end up suffering due to our uncontrolled appetites. Lord have mercy!

We need to remind ourselves that life is too precious to play around with. Let us avoid making unwise decisions that we will live to regret or that will shorten our life on earth.

A Famine like No Other

If there is one book that many people don't have the time for, then it must be the Bible. There is no question that many homes have it stalked on the shelves or somewhere else. But that is about it. Both Christians and non-Christians have no time for this great book that has over the years transformed the lives of millions and given hope to the hopelessness. Equally true, is the fact that many people can find time to go to work, watch TV, visit nightclubs and entertainment facilities but always have an excuse as to why they cannot go to church to worship and praise God. They are always ready to justify themselves or defend the status quo.

Many of us have no time for the things of God. If any subject comes up should it be politics, how to become rich or sex, I bet many people will have something to say. That is not so with the word of God. Perhaps the one key that is mostly used as regards the word of God is the delete key. If anything, the only other time when people have time to say anything about the things of God then that time is when they are writing something negative, to oppose, or make light of the word of God. All these are known to the Lord of the universe.

But know what? What? Time is coming when men, women, young, old, rich, and poor, from every corner of the world, will experience an acute shortage of the word of God. According to the sure word of God, time is coming when people will run here and there in search of the word of God, the ministers and the churches but by then, it will be too late. They will not find it. Here is what the Bible says:

> *"The days are coming," declares the Sovereign LORD," when I will send a famine through the land— not a famine of food or a thirst for water, but a famine of hearing the words of the LORD. Men will stagger from sea to sea and*

wander from north to east, searching for the word of the LORD, but they will not find it. "In that day the lovely young women and strong young men will faint because of thirst. (Amos 8:11-13)

And so what is the solution? "Seek the LORD while he may be found; call on him while he is near" (Isaiah 55:6)

"Blessed are those who hunger and thirst for righteousness, for they will be filled." (Mathew 5:6)

Heavenly Father, I thirst to know your word. Please help me to dwell underneath the cross and learn from you about the plan of salvation. Amen.

What Happened To Respect?

It's rather sad that my parents are not here with us. They rest in their graves waiting for the resurrection morning. I will always be thankful for the way they brought us, their children up. They taught us valuable lessons that personally have guided me all the years of my life.

Among the many lessons that they taught us was the virtue of respect; respect for God and Holy things, elders, teachers, and in fact everybody. Over the years, life has taken me to many places and brought me in contact with people from all walks of life. In my contact with all, I have maintained respect for both young and old, male and female, rich and poor, and many others.

However, it seems as if some people took respect and dumped it into a dustbin. And because of that, they are without it. Following is what I have noticed:

1. Some children have no respect whatsoever towards their parents. They all started well when they were young, but as they grew up, went to school, interacted with others, they decided to disrespect their own parents who brought them up and provided for all their needs without any reservation whatsoever. They would rather respect everyone else but their own parents. What a shame!
2. Some people have no respect whatsoever for God, the Bible, God's temple, and God's servants. They treat all these as common and as deserving no respect.
3. Many employees have no respect for their bosses (Manager or supervisor). Some have lost their jobs for lack of respect.

4. Some spouses have no respect towards their own partners. They yell at them, call them names, and humiliate them in the presence of children and/or others.
5. Many people do not respect themselves. Some of the things they write, say and do leave a lot to be desired. Someone needs to re-educate them
6. When asking for some financial assistance of any kind, some lack the sense of asking. How so? In a way, they despise the very person that they need their help from. This has indeed become a stumbling block in assisting those in needy.

It might help some of us to go back to the way we were brought up. I am almost certain that all parents teach their children the virtue of respect. If you don't mind, go through their notes again and remember that respect for God, Holy things and God's children is a must have virtue.

I will surely hold on to this virtue and promise to use it as long as I am alive. We all need it, or so I think.

A Disease Called Pride

Pride is a disease that is known to destroy its victims and separate them from the rest of the world. Once it infects someone, it elevates its victims to a position whereby they think that they are better than anyone else. It leads to an attitude of knowing it. No wonder the Bible tells us that" Pride goes before destruction, a haughty spirit before a fall. (Proverbs 16:18) It was pride that led to the fall of Lucifer, the morning star. The same disease has led and continues to lead to the l downfall of many. What are the symptoms of the victims of pride?

1. They feel like they are at the top of the world or roof.
2. They feel like only their ideas/opinions count. They are too arrogant to accept or buy other people's ideas.
3. They are always right.
4. Some of them have come to entertain the thought that after all, they can do without God. They don't recognize God. Lord, have mercy!

And what leads to this disease? It includes but is not limited to:

1. Beauty. Even though beauty is in the eyes of the beholder, some somehow feel they are more beautiful/ handsome than others. Such can be very arrogant indeed.
2. Education. Some of those who get good grades at school or happen to be attending famous schools have oftentimes carried an attitude of arrogance. The same applies to some of those who have been privileged to go to graduate and postgraduate schools.
3. Change of social status. Many are not able to handle fame, wealth or change of social status.

In a nutshell, this disease called fame unless checked, can lead to permanent isolation between the victim and God, loved ones and friends. Except for rare cases, most victims of this disease happen to know it or have heard others talk or complain about it.

Here's what the good Lord requires of each one of us:

"Let not the wise man boast of his wisdom or the strong man boast of his strength or the rich man boast of his riches, but let him who boasts boast about this: that he understands and knows me, that I am the LORD, who exercises kindness, justice and righteousness on earth, for in these I delight," declares the LORD." (Jeremiah 9:23-24)

Well, I don't know about you, but as for me, I pray that the good Lord will cleanse this destructive disease from my system. Even so dear Lord, do it today and not tomorrow

Too Busy To Serve God

That life is just too busy is a fact that is well known to most people, more especially the working class and students. In trying to do it all, many have unfortunately had their priorities mixed up. How so? Many have narrowed their daily schedules to work, studies and/or having a good time. But with what outcome?

1. Stress
2. Burned out
3. Depression
4. Stomach ulcers
5. Regular visits to the hospital and unfortunately death

God, who created us, has always had a formula which if followed; we will have satisfaction and happiness always. Therefore, if you want to succeed, then please follow God's outline. How does it look like?

1. God first, last and best in our lives. Here is how Jesus put it" But seek first his kingdom and his righteousness, and all these things will be given to you as well. Therefore, do not worry about tomorrow, for tomorrow will worry about itself. Each day has enough trouble of its own. (Mathew 6:33-34). What does this mean? Create time to study the Bible, pray and go to church every week.
2. Find time and rest.
3. Find a time and be with your family (spouse, children, relatives, or people who will have a positive impact in your life).

Reflect on this story if you can. A rich fellow suddenly fell sick. He was rushed to the hospital. After a thorough examination, the doctor announced the result. "Your problem is that you are not eating," said the Doctor." I am too busy to eat" answered the rich fellow. The Doctor looked at him and warned," If you don't have time to eat, you will have time to die."

So, to you, I say, "If you are too busy and don't have time to serve God, then you will have time to be stressed up, depressed, burned out and unfortunately to die." The choice is ours. How you choose this day.

Heavenly Father, please forgive us for our foolishness. Many times, we cheat ourselves that we can do it without you. Please open our eyes so that we can see. Amen.

Terminal Illness

Indeed, this world is full of sorrow. If the good Lord allowed me to choose which way I would prefer to die, I'll happily choose to die in my sleep. The least will be to die of a terminal illness. Everything related to battling with a terminal illness is very painful to say the very least. The pain, the mental and physical torture, the loneliness, the hopelessness, the waiting, the money spent, and what have you is just too much for both the patient and those who love him or her.

I have seen it all with some of my family members, relatives, friends, and church members. I have stood there crying and doing everything possible to assure them of our God's tender love/care and yet nothing seems to make sense at such times. I am sick and tired of this good for nothing world. I just want to go home; I mean the home of the saved. I pray every single day to be found worthy of being a citizen there.

To all those who have gone through the ordeal of terminal illness in the family and for those who might be going through it even as I write, please know for a fact that all this will come to pass. So, journey on trusting and counting on the many and numerous promises of our loving heavenly father. My prayers and thoughts are with you.

Hmmm, this world is just painful. One day at a time is all that I am asking for.

Cheers fellow travelers. Soon we'll be home.

Lead Us Not Into Temptation

The Bible presents God as one who is always there to protect and shield His children from harm and danger. He does this by either sending His angels or at times by being there in person. In the words of the Psalmist, "The angel of the LORD encamps around those who fear him, and he delivers them" (Psalms 34:7).

It was with this kind of confidence that David further penned these encouraging words.

> *"The LORD is my shepherd; I shall not be in want. He makes me lie down in green pastures; he leads me beside quiet waters, he restores my soul. He guides me in paths of righteousness for his name's sake. Even though I walk through the valley of the shadow of death, I will fear no evil, for you are with me; your rod and your staff, they comfort me. You prepare a table before me in the presence of my enemies. You anoint my head with oil; my cup overflows. Surely goodness and love will follow me all the days of my life, and I will dwell in the house of the LORD forever." (Psalms 23:1-6)*

Much as our God is always there for us, wisdom is needed in identifying danger and fleeing away from it. In other words, we must flee from the territory where Satan and his agents are known to be. James concurs when he writes: "Submit yourselves, then, to God. Resist the devil, and he will flee from you. Come near to God and he will come near to you" (James 4:7-8) But is that always the case? I am afraid not. How so?

Many of us either willingly or foolishly drive ourselves into forbidden areas or worse still the enemy territory and once there, expect God to perform a miracle and rescue us. Jesus advised against this in His teaching on the Lord's Prayer. He taught, "And lead us not into temptation, but deliver us from the evil one" (Mathew 6:13). The message here is that we must avoid driving ourselves into temptation.

It reminds me of two stories; one which I read and another one told. I once read about this priest who one day decided to walk into a bar just to be with his friends. As he was there minding his business, the devil tempted him to indulge in drinking. He confronted the devil by wondering how he would dare tempt the man of the cloth. The devil's message was loud and clear." How come you are in my territory?" wondered the devil. The man of the cloth left speechless.

The story I heard was about this pastor who one day decided to make his own airplane without any wiring or applying mechanical knowledge. Once done, he climbed a big tree carrying his airplane anticipating a miracle. Once on the top of the tree, he entered into his airplane and jumped from one of its branches. As you can imagine, he badly hurt himself.

As a baby, our Lord and Savior-Jesus Christ faced too many challenges. Chief among them was the attempt by King Herod to kill Him due to his political ambition. Mathew chapter two tells us the steps that God took to protect His son. Let us read on:

"When they had gone, an angel of the Lord appeared to Joseph in a dream, "Get up," he said, "take the child and his mother and escape to Egypt. Stay there until I tell you, for Herod is going to search for the child to kill him." (Mathew 2:13) What? Flee to Egypt? Yes, you read right. Even though our God has all the power, He did not desire to be at the enemy camp. Was that all? No, God continued to give more directions/commands. Read on:

"After Herod died, an angel of the Lord appeared in a dream to Joseph in Egypt and said, "Get up, take the child and his mother and go to the land of Israel, for those who were trying to take the child's life are dead." So he got up, took the child and his mother, and went to the land of Israel. But when he heard that Archelaus was reigning in Judea in place of his father Herod, he was afraid to go there. Having been warned in a dream, he withdrew to the district of Galilee, and he went and lived in a town called Nazareth. So was fulfilled what was said through the prophets: "He will be called a Nazarene" (Mathew 2:19-23).

If such were the steps that the good Lord took to protect His son, it only goes to warn all of us to avoid the enemy territory. Seeing that the enemy does not fear or respect anyone let us all do whatever it takes to flee from the enemy and his many attacks.

The Very Silent God

In the category of the Biblical characters that I love and admire, can be found the names of Zachariah, the priest, and his dear wife-Elizabeth-. Note how beautifully the Bible describes them:

"In the time of Herod king of Judea there was a priest named Zechariah, who belonged to the priestly division of Abijah; his wife Elizabeth was also a descendant of Aaron. Both were upright in the sight of God, observing the entire Lord's commandments and regulations blamelessly (Luke 1:5-6)

Like all human beings, this Godly couple had a challenging issue. Which one? "But they had no children because Elizabeth was barren, and they were both well along in years." (Luke 1:7)

I have a feeling that they presented their petition so many times and somewhere due to the prolonged silence by the living God, they either gave up or forgot about it without complaining or cursing God as it's the manner of many of us. But did God forget about this God-fearing couple? No sir!

Even though God appeared to be silent, He was waiting for His fullness of time. And when that time came, He sent His angel to announce the good news. Here it's!

"Then an angel of the Lord appeared to him, standing at the right side of the altar of incense. When Zechariah saw him, he was startled and was gripped with fear. But the angel said to him: "Do not be afraid, Zechariah; your prayer has been heard. Your wife Elizabeth will bear you a son, and you are to give him the name John. He will be a joy and

delight to you, and many will rejoice because of his birth, for he will be great in the sight of the Lord. He is never to take wine or other fermented drink, and he will be filled with the Holy Spirit even from birth. Many of the people of Israel will he bring back to the Lord their God. And he will go on before the Lord, in the spirit and power of Elijah, to turn the hearts of the fathers to their children and the disobedient to the wisdom of the righteous—to make ready a people prepared for the Lord."(Luke 1:11-17)

Oh, I truly love this story for it has been a source of encouragement to me for many years. It did the miracle when my wife and I did not have children for 4 long years. It did the miracle in my many years of struggling to send myself to college/University. And yes it did the miracle when I recently started working as a full-time minister in the Minnesota conference. I have had to wait upon the Lord even when He appeared to have disappeared.

The words of my favorite author-Ellen G White -say it all," Our God has got a thousand and one ways to provide for the needs of His children of which we know none." Thank you, Jesus! Therefore, Cheer up fellow travelers. He who is on our side-even the Lord Jesus-is greater than many of us realize. Smile and move on in great confidence and faith in the living God."

What about death?

Do you know that someday you will die? Any plans for that yet? What about plans for your funeral service, burial place, and any other? Do you have a will all written and signed?

It's rather interesting to note that while many take pains to prepare for a better life tomorrow, a good number of us don't want to think about it leave alone talking and planning for it. This is so even though," For the living know that they will die," (Ecclesiastes 9:5).

Even though no one knows neither the day nor the hour of our death, it's very clear that we'll die someday due to accident, disease/sickness, hunger/famine, homicide, suicide, old age, and who knows what?

Whenever some people suddenly pass on, a lot of stuff has surfaced that has caused more division, hatred, fighting and in some cases, the court has been called upon to help decide? Why? This is because while the individual was alive, he or she avoided or neglected to make certain decisions. Like which ones?

1. If you live in the city, Diaspora or are married to a different tribe/race, then you must make it very clear as to where you will want to be buried.
2. If you have property, then make a will that will express your desire of who gets what.
3. If you are married, then let your spouse know what is where and all other financial transactions.
4. If you have children, then see to it that everything you own is divided among your children and spouse.
5. If you are in Diaspora and wish to be buried there, then start thinking of insurance that will take care of burial expenses

And perhaps the greatest preparation that you need to make is to make sure that you have a good relationship with your God; one that will secure you a place among the saints at the resurrection morning.

Two things that we should all avoid, is to deceive ourselves that we will be around for some time and therefore ignore all kinds of preparation. Another temptation that we need to avoid is that of leading a careless life devoid of God and then deceiving ourselves that something will be done after we die. The Bible presents that time as now as opposed to later.

So what plans have you made concerning your death? If death visited you today, will it find you ready?

Even so, Lord Jesus teaches us to number our days.

The Sin of Criticism

Let me start by making it known that I am for constructive criticism; the kind that not only appreciates the little that others have done but also suggests meaningful solutions that help the concerned person to succeed. But as it is, some people have majored in criticizing others. Look at the following:

1. There are people who love to criticize the Bible, the church, the church leaders, the church doctrines and anything Godly just for the fun of it.
2. There are spouses who are always out to criticize their partners. Nothing he or she does makes sense.
3. There are people who have never written a book but are quick to criticize those who have ventured to put their thoughts on paper. Why can't they instead show a good example by writing a best seller book since they know the language and what is acceptable?
4. There are those who spend all their time criticizing certain leaders. All they think about is how to make their boss or a certain leader look bad.

All need to remember that destructive criticism destroys others and hinders the progress that others aspire to do. Criticism takes the view that whoever is doing it is better than the accused. Sounds like the work of the devil and indeed translates into sin. How does God regard such kind of behavior? He abhors it. I will cite some biblical evidence. Remember Moses and his siblings (Aaron and Miriam?" One day, Miriam took it upon herself to criticize Moses. God's reaction tells it all. Read on:

"Miriam and Aaron began to talk against Moses because of his Cushite wife, for he had married a Cushite. "Has the LORD spoken only through Moses?" they asked. "Hasn't he

also spoken through us?" And the LORD heard this. (Now Moses was a very humble man, humbler than anyone else on the face of the earth.) At once the LORD said to Moses, Aaron, and Miriam, "Come out to the Tent of Meeting, all three of you." So, the three of them came out. Then the LORD came down in a pillar of cloud; he stood at the entrance to the Tent and summoned Aaron and Miriam. When both stepped forward, he said, "Listen to my words: "When a prophet of the LORD is among you, I reveal myself to him in visions, I speak to him in dreams. But this is not true of my servant Moses; he is faithful in my entire house. With him I speak face to face, clearly and not in riddles; he sees the form of the LORD. Why then were you not afraid to speak against my servant Moses?"

The anger of the LORD burned against them, and he left them. When the cloud lifted from above the Tent, there stood Miriam—leprous, like snow. Aaron turned toward her and saw that she had leprosy; and he said to Moses, "Please, my lord, do not hold against us the sin we have so foolishly committed." (Numbers 12:1-11)

So, before we open our mouths, or sit behind the keyboard to criticize anything, let us think twice. God who knows our inner motives has a way of dealing with such issues. Let us, therefore, tread very carefully.

Two Kinds of Death

The Bible talks about 2 kinds of death (the death of a saint and the death of a sinner); one is precious before the eyes of God and the other one is very painful indeed. How do you mean?

Ecclesiastes 9:5 reads," For the living know that they will die, but the dead know nothing; they have no further reward, and even the memory of them is forgotten." Yes, unfortunately, due to the original sin, all human beings will die someday. So, whether you like it or not and regardless of your status, someday, you will have to say goodbye to this world.

Regarding the death of a saint or those who have fully surrendered their lives unto the creator of the universe, the Bible states, " Precious in the sight of the LORD is the death of his saints." (Psalms 116:15). Why precious? Here is what the Bible teaches,

> *"Do not be amazed at this, for a time is coming when all who are in their graves will hear his voice and come out— those who have done good will rise to live, and those who have done evil will rise to be condemned" (John 5:28-29.)*

> *"But I would not have you to be ignorant, brethren, concerning them which are asleep, that ye sorrow not, even as others which have no hope. For if we believe that Jesus died and rose again, even so, them also which sleep in Jesus wills God to bring with him. For this, we say unto you by the word of the Lord, that we which are alive and remain unto the coming of the Lord shall not prevent them which are asleep. For the Lord, himself shall descend from heaven with a shout, with the voice of the archangel, and with the*

trump of God: and the dead in Christ shall rise first: Then we which are alive and remain shall be caught up together with them in the clouds, to meet the Lord in the air: and so, shall we ever be with the Lord. Wherefore comfort one another with these words." (1 Thessalonians 4:13-18)

So, if by the time of one passing, he or she had already chosen Jesus Christ as his or her personal Savior, then there is no cause for alarm. Such a person has gone to sleep awaiting the resurrection morning. Hallelujah. The kind of death that makes God sad and one that we all need to avoid is the death of a sinner. Our God is not interested in the death of a sinner. The Bible states:" Do I take any pleasure in the death of the wicked? declares the Sovereign LORD. Rather, am I not pleased when they turn from their ways and live? (Ezekiel 18:23).

If by the time of his or her death one had not set things right with his or her creator, then such is a sealed case. In other words, there is no atonement or redemption to a dead sinner. No not according to the Bible. That is why you and I need to surrender our lives daily; daily because we have no idea when our lives on earth will come to an end.

With a determined effort to see many lost forever, the devil deceives millions such that death catches them totally unaware. But you and I need not die as sinners. The good Lord wants to live with us for eternity. It's up to us to choose which kind of death we'll die.

Even so Lord Jesus, please let me die as a saint. Help me to live each day as if it were my last day on earth. Amen and amen! How about you?

Who Is Right; God Or Us?

I know that many of us are authorities in many areas of life. Whenever we speak, we do so with unquestionable authority. But when it comes to the things of God, God is the ultimate authority. Whatever He says will stand the test of time no matter what any mortal human being will say or do. What I do not understand is why we being humans think that we can alter that which the Lord of the universe has stated in a language so clear. Just take a look at the following and tell me who we think we are.

1. God tells us that it took Him six days to create this world (Exodus 20:6). But we teach that we were not created by God but then happen to be here by the process of evolution.
2. God tells us that He rested on the 7th day of the week and therefore all must remember the Sabbath day to keep it holy. (Genesis 2:2-3; Exodus 20:8-11). But we teach that we can choose any day and declare it holy. Wait a minute who gave us that authority?
3. God tells us that when someone dies, he/she returns to the ground until the resurrection day when all those who are in the graves will hear His voice and come forth John 5:28-29) But we teach that one a person dies, he or she turns into an angel. What?
4. God tells us that the Bible is His Holy word and that the writers were inspired by Him (2 Peter 1:20-21: 2 Timothy 3:15-17). But we teach that the Bible is one of the many good books. Now that is so contrary to what God says.

There are so many things that we teach that are so contrary to what God has told us. It will be nice to remember that God warns all those who twist His word and teach it so. Here's what He says:

> *"Do not think that I have come to abolish the Law or the Prophets; I have not come to abolish them but to fulfill them. I tell you the truth, until heaven and earth disappear, not the smallest letter, not the least stroke of a pen; will by any means disappear from the Law until everything is accomplished. Anyone who breaks one of the least of these commandments and teaches others to do the same will be called least in the kingdom of heaven, but whoever practices and teaches these commands will be called great in the kingdom of heaven" (Mathew 5:17-19)*

Help Answer Your Prayers

Every single day, we send our petitions to our loving, forgiving, merciful, and caring heavenly father. Every time we do that, He answers in one of the three ways: No; Wait: Yes! Come to think about it, there are some prayers that we can help by answering. Here are my thoughts:

1. We can help by choosing what we watch/see, listen to, eat, drink, read, and how we think.
2. We can help by choosing whom to hang around with and the places that we hang around.
3. We can help by going out to find a job than just sitting and waiting for a miracle to happen.
4. We can choose by letting go of our weaknesses and letting Jesus into our lives.
5. We can help by choosing obedience instead of disobedience.
6. We can choose to be free or be slaves forever.
7. We can choose to accept help or just sit there crying

Bottom line is that we have a very crucial part to play. Find out what it's and work on it. Shall we?

In Defense of the Devil

Any time anyone has been caught in the very act of committing a sin or breaking the law, the blame has always been on Satan/the devil. If the devil was called upon to defend himself, I am pretty sure that he will blame the victims and not himself. How come? You see from time immemorial; the devil's motive has been and remains the same. From the time he rebelled in heaven (Isaiah 14:12-18; Ezekiel 28:11-19; Revelation 12:7-9) he got himself a job to deceive, misrepresent God, His law, and to destroy all, more particularly those who are called by the name of Christ. To accomplish his mission, he has done everything possible to attract, if possible, the whole world into him.

A careful study of the word of God reveals the work of the devil. Let us pull out from the Biblical archives those passages that tell us that which he has done and done it openly.

1. He told the first lie and succeeded in deceiving Adam and Eve (Genesis 3:4-5).
2. He told God that his work was to move freely in the world and accused God of protecting Job. He challenged God to allow him to test Job. Thank God that Job came out victorious. (Job 1:6-11).
3. The gospels tell us that the devil not only wanted to kill the infant Jesus but gave Him hard time all the time He was on earth. He finally led his agents to crucify Jesus on the cross as a criminal.
4. Mathew 7:13-14 tells us that Satan is the leader of the wider gate that leads to destruction.
5. Jesus warned Peter that the devil was out to destroy him.

"Simon, Simon, Satan has asked to sift all of you as wheat. But I have prayed for you, Simon that your faith may not

fail. And when you have turned back, strengthen your brothers (Luke 22:31-32).

1. His mission is to destroy, if possible, all. Listen to Peter,

" Be alert and of sober mind. Your enemy the devil prowls around like a roaring lion looking for someone to devour." (1 Peter 5:8).

So, really the problem is not with the devil but us. Why do you say that? Well, if someone makes it very clear to you that his mission is to deceive, destroy/kill you, why will you want to follow such a person.The challenge with many of us is as follows:

1. We fail to watch and pray that we don't enter temptation.
2. We love the devil, his agents, and programs.
3. Even though we know that he is our greatest enemy, we still allow him to dwell in our hearts and our homes.
4. We hate with passion all those (pastors and Christ's followers) who warn us of the many snares/tricks of the enemy.
5. We want to please both God and the enemy at the same time. This cannot work by all means

So, why do we befriend the devil and his agents and then turn around and blame them?

Who is to blame; we or the devil?

If You Love Someone

Each one of us claims to love someone (wife, husband, children, parents, friends, leaders, siblings, school/college mates, Jesus/God) at one time or the other. While such claims might mean something else to different people, there are certain things that support such claims. Like what? If you truly love someone and you mean it, then:

1. You must prove it
2. You must be there for your friend in times of happiness and in times of sorrow.
3. You must spend quality time with such a person. Do you love Jesus/God? If you do, here is what He expects of all those who make such claims:
4. Jesus said," If you love me, you will keep my commandments" (John 14:15)
5. John wrote" For this is the love of God, that we keep His commandments; and His commandments are not burdensome.
6. We must spend time with Him praying for ourselves and others
7. We must avoid the temptation of skipping church meetings and instead form a habit of joining fellow believers as we learn from them and encourage them. Here is how Paul puts it: "Let us not give up meeting together, as some are in the habit of doing, but let us encourage one another—and all the more as you see the Day approaching." (Hebrews 10:25)
8. We must spend time not just reading but studying the word and be willing to go by what it commands. Help is always available to those who need it:" If any of you

lacks wisdom, he should ask God, who gives generously to all without finding fault, and it will be given to him." (James 1:5

9. We must do everything possible to promote His work on earth. Let it be our desire to support the Lord's work near and far. Let us use the God given resources wisely and responsively.

So, do you really love Jesus? Then let us walk the talk. I am willing to do that at whatever cost. I am sure that you too or am I just making an assumption?

The Silent God Part 2

Many over the centuries have wondered and even questioned God's silence especially when they need Him most. Many will tell you that they have prayed over certain issues for so long until they gave up.

I just wanted to remind ourselves that our God is not all that silent as some of us allege. On the contrary, even when we think that He is silent, He is actively involved in fighting the evil forces, reorganizing things and removing the roadblocks to answer our petitions. So, when you think that He is silent, know that He has your interests in His heart and will surely come back to you at the fullness of time with exciting news.

Do you recall Abraham, the father of faith? After he repeatedly presented what seemed to him to be a huge mountain, the Sovereign God promised to do something about it. What followed was a silence that took 25 years. In other words, God appeared as if He disappeared. But guess what? 25 years to the dot, God at the appointed time fulfilled His promise! What an awesome God we serve! Note how Sarah reacted:

> *"Now the LORD was gracious to Sarah as he had said, and the LORD did for Sarah what he had promised. Sarah became pregnant and bore a son to Abraham in his old age, at the very time God had promised him. Abraham gave the name Isaac to the son Sarah bore him. When his son Isaac was eight days old, Abraham circumcised him, as God commanded him. Abraham was a hundred years old when his son Isaac was born to him.*
>
> *Sarah said, "God has brought me laughter, and everyone who hears about this will laugh with me." And she added,*

"Who would have said to Abraham that Sarah would nurse children? Yet I have borne him a son in his old age." (Genesis 21:1-6).

Listen, whatever your challenges are in life or right now, rest assured that our heavenly father loves all His children and that He is always on time in answering the prayers of each one of them. Do you mind waiting?

My Sincere Advice to the Youth

Hello young people,

The future of any nation, church, and the success of any institution/organization depend on you. God knows this, both the political and religious leaders know this, your parents know this, you know this and unfortunately, the devil also knows this. And so as you grow up, the world as it were is going to bombard you with so many challenges: If you can, reflect on the following:

1. The good Lord has been in the business of finding honest, sincere, faithful, respectful, trustworthy young people to spread the good news and become an influence to the other young people; young people who can spend time daily studying the word and seeking for wisdom that comes from above. Young people who will be like Joseph in Egypt; Daniel, Shadrack, Abednego, and Meshack in Babylon. Will you be that young person?
2. The church needs young people who amidst the many daily challenges have chosen to leave the world alone and follow the Lord Jesus in all that they do. Can the church depend on you?
3. Your parents who have brought you this far and have worked hard and did everything possible to provide for your daily needs will want to see you succeed in your education, get a good job and take part in your marriage and in bringing up their grandchildren. Besides God, your parents have been the closest to you. They have taken God's place in instructing you and teaching you to differentiate between the good and the evil forces. Never at any time disappoint your parents or cut off your relationship with them. If we are in this world, you are

definitely going to need your parents in one way or the other. Let no one deceive you that you can do it alone. That will be the gravest mistake that you will ever make. Be careful young people for this world is full of sorrows. You can't do it alone.

4. The devil and his agents are also interested with you; for what?

He plans to destroy and even kill you. The devil is going to use several and various sources to get you. He is known to have used such over the years to destroy the young people. Like which ones? (Friends, relatives, schoolmates, colleagues, the community, and the entertainment industry). In all that you do, remember that God and your parents have your interest in their hearts. You may cut off your relationship with all others if you chose to but you can't cut your relationship with God and your parents and hope to succeed.

Anyone, therefore (Aunties, uncles, friends, boyfriend/girlfriend and the enemy) who will attempt to deceive and take you away from your parents must be ignored by all means. Listen to me. Let no one cheat you by promising that they will always be there for you. Many have been cheated and abandoned. Only parents can promise that and indeed keep that promise.

Never at any time ignore your parent's advice or do anything without their blessing. Those who have done it will plead with you never even attempt it. Watch your move very carefully and never at any time think that you are now wiser than your parents.

Any time you find yourself in conflict with your parents, please spend more time on your knees and never cut yourself from your parents.

Well, my prayers and thoughts are with you young people. Seek the wisdom that comes from above and you will never regret

Who Oversees Your Home?

It's rather sad that some men who were appointed as the head of their families by God Himself have miserably failed. By failing to do that which the head of the family is supposed to do (act as a priest of his home) by leading/directing his family in great humility and the fear of God, they have relinquished their responsibilities to someone else but them. So then who is in charge?

1. In some homes, the man's family members (brother, sister, parents) are in total control. These men are just there to follow whatever these relatives say.
2. In some homes, the in-laws are in solid control. All these men do is sing any song taught by the in-laws. In some homes, friends are in charge of everything. They are known to call the sorts.
3. To fill the vacuum/gap in some homes, children and some wives have been forced to jump into the steering wheel and drive on the car to maybe its final destination

How come that some men have failed their responsibilities? There would be other factors but the following is what I have found out.

1. By denying Jesus Christ as the head of their families, these men have forsaken the only expert in the family affairs
2. By failing to provide for their families, they have reduced their power and influence. All they can do is just bark but have no teeth to bite.
3. Due to drinking and abuse of drugs, they lack the ability to guide/lead by example.
4. Other stuff has taken their priorities.

Please note that any time leadership lacks in any family/community, each person does his own things or people get lost. The following two passages say so. Read on.

"In those days Israel had no king; all the people did whatever seemed right in their own eyes." (Judges 17:6)

"Where [there is] no vision, the people perish: but he that keeps the law, happy [is] he." (Proverbs 29:18)

Some men need to wake up from their slumber and provide the needed leadership. To succeed, they need to depend on the Lord of the universe and use the Bible as the more reliable source. Come on my tribe (men) let us carry on our God given responsibilities in great humility following the pattern laid down by our God. But if you feel like you lack the power and will, then allow your dear wife and children to help out. In such a situation, learn to talk less and follow as directed.

It will definitely help to read and reflect on this passage," Submit to one another out of reverence for Christ. Wives, submit yourselves to your own husbands as you do to the Lord. For the husband, is the head of the wife as Christ is the head of the church, his body, of which he is the Savior. Now as the church submits to Christ, so also wives should submit to their husbands in everything. Husbands, love your wives, just as Christ loved the church and gave himself up for her" (Ephesians 5:21-25).

Let us make sure that we don't read into this passage. Let us not force it to say what it was not meant to say.

Things That We Must Not Tamper With

Every time I read the daily papers/magazine, watch, or listen to the news, I cannot help but conclude that something is definitely a miss! We have gone too far that unless we are careful, I am afraid that we might end up suffering the consequences!

Whether knowingly or unknowingly, we are treading on very dangerous ground! But first, let us start with that which we know and can relate to!

In our dealing with one another, I am sure that you have heard at one time or the other the following expressions:

1. You are stepping on my last nerve!
2. I was pushed to the corner!
3. I am coming to a point of no return!

Any time you hear such expressions, you better stay off otherwise something unthinkable might happen!

But what about our God! History reveals that there comes a time when God says enough is enough! Here are some examples!

1. Genesis Chapter 11 tells us that there was a time when human beings embarked on a project of building the tower of Babel with the intent to reach God. At the time when they thought that they were making progress, God came down and confused their languages, thus dealing them a humiliating blow!
2. Genesis chapter 19 tells us that there was a time that God would not tolerate their madness. He, therefore, destroyed the cities of Sodom and Gomorrah

3. In Exodus chapter 3, God was so unhappy with the way Pharaoh, the king of Egypt, was treating His people that he decided to intervene and set them free!

What about our time and age? The same God declares loud and very clear "Be not deceived; God is not mocked: for whatsoever a man soweth, that shall he also reap!" Galatians 6:7

Based on the word of God, there are several things that human beings should not and must not tamper with. I will highlight five of those.

A failure to respect these five or stop tampering with them may as well be the reason for our sufferings. You see when it comes to the things of God, the solution has always been and will be to follow "Thus says the Lord!

Here are the five as the Bible presents them:

1. The good Lord did not leave us without enough instruction on what to do in matters of worship. The book of Genesis tells us that God Himself rested not on any day, but one day during the week. Mark you that He blessed that day and declared it His day of worship. In the book of exodus chapter 20, he admonishes us to remember that day to keep it Holy. Friends, let us go by what the Bible tells us and not on how we feel.
2. Life originated from God and must be respected by all. We must not take part in taking anybody's life for whatsoever reason. Security in many parts of the world has deteriorated so badly that many live in great fear.
3. Let us respect God's money and stop using it any way we feel. God has given us enough instruction on what is ours and what belongs to Him.

4. The Bible is a sure word of God. It's not a toy that anybody can play with. Let us handle it with care! Pray for the wisdom and understanding that comes from above to help you understand and appreciate it!

We need to take time, research on the above five and do as the Lord wants.

God's Delete Key!

At the time of designing a computer, the designer/s thought it a wise idea to include among other major keys, a delete key. This is the one key that has either been used properly or misused. This key has helped many to get rid of the junk e-mail which to some, come in thousands. In this way, it has given a breathing space to the in box. It also helps get rid of the unwanted draft copies and clear the sent/bulk/trash boxes.

That said, this key has brought mental torture and frustration to many people. How so? People have accidentally touched this key thus whipping off needed information, such as a term paper, thesis, or dissertation. At such moments, some have felt that this key was included by mistake. Further, some delete anything they see or messages that would have been of great help to them.

Since I have been a victim of this key, I have learned to use it wisely. Maybe I should pause and ask: What's your take on the delete key? Whether anyone needs this key or not, would be a good subject of debate, but I am not going to dwell on it anymore

I now want to shift to another delete key that I value a great deal-God's delete key! I don't know about you, but many are the times I have disappointed and caused pain to my heavenly father. Every time I realize my foolishness, I have always found myself at the feet of the merciful Savior. Indeed, He has always accepted me by simply using the delete key to wipe all my foolishness/sins.

Listen to how He puts it:

"Praise the LORD, o my soul, and forget not all his benefits who forgives all your sins and heals all your diseases." (Psalms 103:2-3.)

"As far as the east is from the west, so far has He removed our transgressions from us." (Psalms 103:12.)

"Come now let us reason together, says the Lord. Though your sins are like scarlet, they will be as white as snow......" (Isaiah 1:18-20.)

"If we confess our sins, He is faithful and just and will forgive us our sins and purify us of all unrighteousness." (1 John 1:9.)

Oh, I truly love and need God's key every single day on my journey home. How about you my friend?

My Four Homes

Since childhood, I have lived in several places that I regarded as my home. Three of those stand out! And the last one is a reality that occupies my mind all day long!

1. My childhood home.
    - I cherish good memories of my childhood home
    - It was clean, well fenced and with maximum security. You had to pass through four gates before you reached our home.
    - You had to be home by 5:00 PM otherwise you would be locked out
2. A very special apartment
    - When I moved to this apartment complex some years back, the owners told me to regard this as my home if I wanted to.
    - Of all the apartments that I have lived at ever since migrating to this great country, this one had maximum security. Some friends even joked by saying that this kind of security was not good for a pastor
    - It was very clean but expensive too!
3. Our retirement homes
    - On September 1st, 2017, we bought the retirement home that we truly love. Everything about it- good neighborhood, security, space and many others is well appreciated.
    - My concern is that assuming Jesus doesn't deem it necessary to return that soon and assuming that I

will be alive, it's going to take us some 30 years to complete paying the mortgage!

4. My heavenly home!

- This is the one home that I find myself dreaming about all the time
- Guess what! It will not be an ordinary home! No! It will be a mansion
- It will be rent free. It shall never be foreclosure! Wow!
- Security will not be an issue
- Everything will be provided by my heavenly father
- The weather will be perfect
- Landscaping will be perfect
- There will be all kinds of flowers and fruits
- I will enjoy watching the birds and all kinds of animals

All I need to do to claim it is to pray, be faithful, and endure to the very end!

By the way, did I tell you that there will be enough homes for all who choose to be there? Check it out in John 14:1-2; Revelation 21:1-4

Would you like to by my neighbor, maybe, live along the same street!

Not Too Late To Turn Around

In all fairness, I cannot claim to be good at directions. I can tell west from East, and North from South. But when you place them together, they no doubt confuse me. And because of this, I have often time given people wrong directions. Whenever they call to say that they are lost, I ask them to turn around and head the right direction; of course, after giving my sincere apologies! Turn around and head in the right direction!

It comes as no surprise to anyone, at least not to me that many are the people who have either chosen on found themselves headed in the wrong direction! Allow me to highlight but a few:

1. There were many people who were happily married at one time. Everything was fine if they remained in the Lord, who by the way is the firm foundation of all marriages. They ignored all words of wisdom and went separate ways! Since the day they separated/divorced, things have gone from worse to worst
2. There are many husbands and wives who as I write are headed the wrong direction. Instead of sitting down, examining each one to see where things went wrong, they have instead justified each other's behavior, actions, attitude and what have you. For a long time, they have left so many minute things unattended to a point that there is so much anger, frustration and a sense of loss and betrayal.
3. There are many people out there who at one time were God-fearing individuals. For some reason, they changed course, stopped going to church or even studying the Bible, chose to work even on the Sabbath and cheated themselves that all was well. The truth of the matter is

that unless they come to themselves and turn around, they are headed south

4. There are many people whose lives are messed up due to the influence of other people. In a desire to become like their peers, they not only chose the wrong company of friends but also chose to behave like them

5. There are many people out there whose lives are totally messed up due to drinking and smoking. Instead of owning up to their bad behavior and accepting to change, they have for a long time now, living a life of denial! Things will get worse unless they chose to turn around!

I can go on and on, but the bottom line is that there are people out there who have headed in the wrong direction. They have been driving in the wrong direction for so long that somehow they have come to tell themselves that after all things will be alright!

Are you one of them or do you know anyone who has headed in the wrong direction! Here is the good news. There is an only one-the man of Galilee who can sure mend broken lives. If you choose to connect with Him today by following His well-written directions, your life will never be the same.

And remember that it's not too late to turn around. The question is am I willing? Are you?

Open the Church Doors

A walk of churches on Saturday/Sunday, will tell you that many of them are dying out; they are closing down due to a lack of members. You can hardly see the young generation there. The majority are sixty and above. And because of this sudden reality, some churches have whether knowingly or unknowingly have found themselves watering down their doctrines. There is very little emphasis on doctrines anymore. The word of God is used as long as it does not affect or annoy anyone. So much has been compromised.

There is no question that the church doors should and must be opened to all for after all we are all sinners and come short of the glory of God. What I think should not be done is to ask people to come the way they are and remain the way they are. There is a need to remind all the difference between God's love towards the sinner and His hatred towards sin. After all, the church is all about God and a sinner and not a fellow human being with another fellow human being.

Any hospital that will open its doors to the sick and yet encourage them to remain sick would have flatly defeated its own purpose or what do you think?

Being Always Right

We all like making our own independent decisions; decisions on what to eat/drink, wear; whom to marry, hang around with; whether to go to school or not, whether to change jobs and many more. There is no question that it takes us time to arrive at such decisions and if anything, once we have decided, some of us don't want to entertain any thoughts on changing it.

I am sure that in trying to advise someone, you have sometimes heard such a response as, "I have made up my mind and will not change it no matter what". Some people are so adamant that they would rather walk away from a job/a marriage or leave home to someone's home than change their" perfect decisions or way of seeing things."

Is there one who is always right? Maybe, but I have yet to find one. Since some decisions are very crucial, those in responsible positions do consultations before arriving at the final decision.

Anyone who refuses to accept any advice and always sees himself/herself as perfect in making such decisions may live to regret it! Are you sure? Many have found themselves in a very awkward situation. As many like to say," experience is the best teacher". Have no problem with that except for the fact that by then, it's always too late.

You know as I do that, we are all human and therefore capable of making mistakes. So, humble yourself and take some advice. Avoid the temptation of dumping every piece of advice into a trash can. Accept the fact that things do go wrong against our so-called perfect plans.

Well, if for any reason, you don't want any human advice, at least consult with the Lord of the universe through prayer. Will you?

Our Own Greatest Enemies

Many of us work/struggle so hard to become our own enemies. By ignoring every piece of advice from our parents, siblings, elders, ministers, spouses, workmates, and the word of God, we venture into some forbidden and dangerous areas that end up destroying us. It's rather pathetic that we ignore the advice of those who love us and instead choose to listen to the wrong people-Those who have failed in life and want someone to accompany them.

Even when you think that you are right or that you know very well the person that you are dealing with, just step back and think again. Avoid the temptation of being naive and acting smart. In the end, you will cry and regret it. Then, all that those who care can offer you is the old comforting phrase of sorry. Plead with the good Lord to help open your eyes so that you can see that which you are ignoring.

Help by stopping today to deepen your own grave. As a matter of fact, stop digging it altogether! Will you?

Mary Magdalene

Here is what the Bible tells us about Mary Magdalene:

1. Luke 7:37-39 A woman in the city who was a sinner, wiped the feet of Jesus with her tears and anointed them with ointment.
2. Luke 8:2 Jesus cast 7 demons out of her.
3. John 11:1-2 she was a sister to Martha and Lazarus and the one who wiped the feet of Jesus.
4. Luke 10:38-42 she sat by Jesus' feet to learn from Him.
5. John 8:1-11 She is believed to be the woman that Jesus forgave," Neither do I condemn thee, go and sin no more."
6. John 20:11-18 she was the first one at the grave on the resurrection morning and the last one to leave.

Here is what others (theologians/scholars/authors) say about her.

At one time, she was a pious God-fearing damsel. Unfortunately, she was led into sin by one religious leader Simon, who was unhappy to see Jesus minister to her. His statement," if this man was a prophet, He would have known what kind of woman is touching her (Luke 7:36-50) says it all.

Ashamed of the life of sin, she left her hometown and resided at Magdala, where she was involved in prostitution. While there, Jesus made her and forgave her. Sadly, she went back to her former life 7 times.

In deepest appreciation for the forgiveness of her sins and the raising of her brother Lazarus, she saved for the whole year and bought a very expensive ointment to anoint Him before His crucifixion.

Mary Magdalene's love for Jesus has always touched and humbled me. Yes, she was forgiven so much and she appreciated it all.

I can't help but wonder," looking back to your life journey, has the Lord Jesus been of any good to you? And what have you done?

God's Undeniable Claims

The Lord of the universe makes very bold and undeniable claims. Let's check them out:

"The earth is the Lord's, and everything in it, the world, and all who live in it." (Psalms 24:1)

"For every animal of the forest is mine, and the cattle on a thousand hills. I know every bird in the mountains, and the creatures of the field are mine." (Psalms 50:10-12)

"The silver is mine and the gold is mine,' declares the LORD Almighty" (Haggai 2:8).

So, who are we in this world? We are but stewards, charged by the Lord of the universe to take care of His creation! Sadly/unfortunately we have made ourselves the owners and made the Lord of all creation a beggar! Just think about that!

There is a need to change our misguided attitude and treat the good Lord the way He deserves. Will you? Even so, help me dear God to realize this.

Pauline Epistles

Anyone preparing for any kind of examination or traveling must not take anything for granted. He or she must make sure that sufficient and reliable information has been gathered, compared and analyzed from all sources. The primary sources and eyewitnesses will play a great role here.

Equally true, in our Christian journey, we must learn not to go by hearsay. Since the Bible is available to us, we must meditatively and prayerfully read and understand it. This is particularly true when we read Pauline's epistles.

There is no question that the apostle Paul is one writer who has been misunderstood/ misread by many. This is more so as regards the law of God. That is why Peter took the pains to point out this misunderstanding. He wrote:

> *"... even as our beloved brother Paul also according to the wisdom given unto him hath written unto you; As also in all his epistles, speaking in them of these things; in which are some things hard to be understood, which they that are unlearned and unstable wrest, as they do also the other scriptures, unto their own destruction (2 Peter 3:15-16).*

Let us not take anything for granted but search for the truth and digest it. A failure to do so will most definitely lead to deep regrets. Then, it will be forever too late. Lord Jesus, please open my eyes so that I can see!

Be Warned

Today, my mind found itself digesting the following passages of Scriptures:

"So, if you think you are standing firm, be careful that you don't fall!"(1 Corinthians 10:12)

"The highway of the upright avoids evil; he who guards his way guards his life. Pride goes before destruction, a haughty spirit before a fall." (Proverbs 16:17-18)

"The heart is deceitful above all things and beyond cure. Who can understand it?" (Jeremiah 17:9)

"Vanity of vanities, says the Preacher; all is vanity." (Ecclesiastes 12:8)

Those who have been endowed with special talents in singing, preaching, administration, or spend more time praying, reading various spiritual books by different authors, and claiming the promises of the Holy Spirit, need not only to read the above Scriptures but also digest and apply them in their daily lives. Why? Because as the apostle Peter warns," Be self-controlled and alert. Your enemy the devil prowls around like a roaring lion looking for someone to devour" (1 Peter 5:8)

Many have focused on their talents to appoint that they have lost sight of Jesus. They have not only disobeyed God's church but also found very little desire to read the word of God. In the end, some have left the faith. Be warned my dear friends for the devil are no respecter of any human being.

Our Attitude Towards Sufferings

Since birth, we have either gone through suffering or know someone (parents, children, siblings, friends, parishioners, pastor, neighbor, colleague, teacher, student or an enemy) who have greatly suffered.

While some have found fault or accused everyone else including God, others have remained strong and steadfast in their faith in the living God or have found refuge in the living God. What ought to be our response/attitude towards suffering? Like in many issues, we'll let the word of God speak to us on this one as well.

> *"If you suffer, it should not be as a murderer or thief or any other kind of criminal, or even as a meddler. However, if you suffer as a Christian, do not be ashamed, but praise God that you bear that name. (1 Peter 4:15-16).*

> *"Though he slays me, yet will I trust in him" (Job 13:15)*

> *"To keep me from becoming conceited because of these surprisingly great revelations, there was given me a thorn in my flesh, a messenger of Satan, to torment me. Three times I pleaded with the Lord to take it away from me. But he said to me, "My grace is sufficient for you, for my power is made perfect in weakness." Therefore, I will boast more gladly about my weaknesses, so that Christ's power may rest on me. That is why, for Christ's sake, I delight in weaknesses, in insults, in hardships, in persecutions, in difficulties. For when I am weak, then I am strong." (2 Corinthians 12:7-10).*

"Who shall separate us from the love of Christ? Shall trouble or hardship or persecution or famine or nakedness or danger or sword? As it is written, "For your sake, we face death all day long; we are considered as sheep to be slaughtered. "No, in all these things we are more than conquerors through him who loved us. For I am convinced that neither death nor life, neither angels nor demons, neither the present nor the future, nor any powers, neither height nor depth, nor anything else in all creation, will be able to separate us from the love of God that is in Christ Jesus our Lord." Romans 8:35-38).

"She said to herself, "If I only touch his cloak, I will be healed." (Mathew 9:21)

"A Canaanite woman from that vicinity came to him, crying out, "Lord, Son of David, have mercy on me! My daughter is suffering terribly from demon possession. "(Mathew 15:22)

"In those days was Hezekiah sick unto death. And Isaiah the Prophet the son of Amoz came unto him, and said unto him, Thus saith the LORD, Set thine house in order: for thou shalt die, and not live. Then Hezekiah turned his face toward the wall, and prayed unto the LORD, And said, Remember now, O LORD, I beseech thee, how I have walked before thee in truth and with a perfect heart, and have done that which is good in thy sight. And Hezekiah wept sore."(Isaiah 38:1-3).

Prayer, faith, and a positive attitude ought to be our attitude.

Closing God's Line of Grace

The Bible states very clearly that ours is a God of love, mercy, long suffering and forgiving. The same Bible tells us that there comes a time when the same God regards certain human behavior/activities as going way too far. Whenever that has happened, He is known to have taken some actions quite contrary to His nature! Come with me as we highlight some of such:

> *"The LORD said, "What have you done? Listen! Your brother's blood cries out to me from the ground. Now you are under a curse and driven from the ground, which opened its mouth to receive your brother's blood from your hand. When you work the ground, it will no longer yield its crops for you. You will be a restless wanderer on the earth." (Genesis 4:10-12)*
>
> *"Then the LORD said, "My Spirit will not contend with man forever, for he is mortal; his days will be a hundred and twenty years." (Genesis 6:3)*
>
> *"So the LORD said, "I will wipe mankind, whom I have created, from the face of the earth—men and animals, and creatures that move along the ground, and birds of the air—for I am grieved that I have made them." (Genesis 6:7)*
>
> *"Then the LORD rained down burning sulfur on Sodom and Gomorrah—from the LORD out of the heavens. Thus he overthrew those cities and the entire plain, including all those living in the cities—and also the vegetation in the land. But Lot's wife looked back, and she became a pillar of salt." (Genesis 19:24-26).*

"Then the LORD said to Moses, "The man must die. The whole assembly must stone him outside the camp." So the assembly took him outside the camp and stoned him to death, as the LORD commanded Moses." (Numbers 15:35-36).

"When they came to the threshing floor of Nacon, Uzzah reached out and took hold of the ark of God, because the oxen stumbled. The Lord's anger burned against Uzzah because of his irreverent act; therefore God struck him down and he died there beside the ark of God. (2 Samuel 6:6-7).

"And he went up from thence unto Bethel: and as he was going up, by the way, there came forth little children out of the city, and mocked him, and said unto him, Go up, thou bald head; go up, thou bald head. And he turned back, and looked on them, and cursed them in the name of the LORD. And there came forth two she bears out of the wood, and tare forty and two children of them." (2 Kings 2:23-24).

"When Ananias heard this, he fell down and died. And great fear seized all who heard what had happened...At that moment she fell down at his feet and died. Then the young men came in and, finding her dead, carried her out and buried her beside her husband. Great fear seized the whole church and all who heard about these events." (Acts 5:5, 10-11).

"On the appointed day Herod, wearing his royal robes, sat on his throne and delivered a public address to the people. They shouted, "This is the voice of a god, not of a man."

Immediately, because Herod did not give praise to God, an angel of the Lord struck him down, and he was eaten by worms and died." (Acts 12:21-23).

These passages just serve as a warning that there comes a time when God says that enough is enough. In all that we do, let us tread carefully lest we close the Lord's line of grace/mercy!

A Slave to a Cell Phone/ Wristwatch

Until last Friday, I did not know or even have the slightest idea that I had become a slave of a cell phone and/or a wristwatch. For some reasons, and unlike me, I lost or should I say I misplaced or forgot my cell phone somewhere, some place most likely at home.

A lone at church, preparing and waiting for the faithful ones to arrive for vespers, I found myself without a cell phone or even a watch. I became restless as I began to imagine the number of people who were trying to get in touch with me. As if that was not enough pain, I had no way of knowing what time it was.

In the end, I learned a very vital lesson; I learned of a need to depend on the Lord Jesus to appoint that I will feel pain and restless to do without Him even for a few moments. I need to train myself not to go anywhere without Him.

My love towards and my dependence upon my Savior ought to be greater than that of a cell phone and/or a wristwatch. Even so, help me dear Lord to realize that.

A Reminder to the World

In these times of great confusion and uncertainty, the world will do well to borrow a leaf from the following passages of the Scriptures:

"but there is a God in heaven" (Daniel 2:28).

"Then the LORD said, "The outcry against Sodom and Gomorrah is so great and their sin so grievous that I will go down and see if what they have done is as bad as the outcry that has reached me. If not, I will know" (Genesis 18:20).

"The LORD said, "I have indeed seen the misery of my people in Egypt. I have heard them crying out because of their slave drivers, and I am concerned about their suffering. And now the cry of the Israelites has reached me, and I have seen the way the Egyptians are oppressing them. (Exodus 3:7, 9).

"The word of the LORD came to Jonah son of Amittai: "Go to the great city of Nineveh and preach against it because its wickedness has come up before me." (Jonah 1:1-2)

"In those days there was no king in Israel; every man did what was right in his own eyes." (Judges 17:6)

"And there is no creature hidden from His sight, but all things are open and laid bare to the eyes of Him with whom we have to do." (Hebrews 4:13).

My people are destroyed for lack of knowledge:" (Hosea 4:6).

Does God see all that is happening in the world today? You bet! Does He care? No doubts whatsoever? The world needs to remember that its salvation lies with the Lord of the universe. Let all who care, sincerely pray that God intervenes and brings hope to those about to give up! I will sure continue to pray for the world and you in particular! Even so, hear my petition oh dear Lord!

Why Guess?

Yesterday, I took a dear friend/new church member, for a new job-related drug test. While waiting, I happened to be reading posters in the office when my eyes landed on one that called for my immediate attention.

It read" Why to guess when you can test?" Its underlined message was to encourage people to go for testing! Testing? What for?

We live in rather very interesting times; times that have witnessed the occurrence of diseases that were not all that common-Cancer, Diabetes, and many others. While some of these diseases are terminal, there are others if caught up at the early stages, can be treated; hence the reason people should go for testing.

As it's, many are afraid of going to see the doctor or to be tested in fear that the unthinkable might be the outcome. And so, whenever they feel some pain, the best they can do is to guess and hope that it will go away.

But even closer to my heart is the guess on whether one is in tune with God or not! Why guess when one has a free thermometer-the Bible, which by the way is free. By use of this God given thermometer, we can gauge our Christian stand in all things of life. I urge all of us to use it to help us understand if we relate to heaven or not. Will you?

A Cargo Without Value

When driving around with my daughter recently, we saw a car that immediately rekindled fond memories. It was Chevy Venture, a 7-seater minivan.

You see a few years ago, we owned a Chevy venture that we all loved. It was among the best cars that we have ever owned. We owned it for 7 years. By the time it died, it still looked like new! Hard to believe that we had to sell it for a mere $ 150.00! Well, it was by all means a throwaway price.

As my daughter and I spoke about it, I would not help but wonder about those things that at one time or the other we hold so dear-money, homes, cars, clothes, positions, education and even our lives? Do you know that a time comes when they all lose their values and don't mean so much?

Just think about this: When one dies, the body becomes of no value. It lays in the mortuary awaiting to be deposed. Some people even fear coming closer to it. When the body is transported by air to its destination, it is marked as, "cargo without value!" Lord, have mercy!

Do we have any lessons here? Yes, let us stop putting too much emphasis/thoughts on things that really don't count. We are living on a borrowed life. Let us, therefore, serve the Lord, who alone means everything to us. Even so, help me dear Lord to focus my attention on you and you alone.

Those Who Wait Upon the Lord

To some, God does not exist period; nothing else will convince them otherwise. They live in their own world void of God. Any mention of God irritates them and is therefore made with resistance and sometimes attack/abuse.

To others, God does exist, but they have nothing to do with Him. He is out there and not all that concerned with their daily struggles. They would rather struggle on their own hoping that somehow things will change for the better by mere luck. The only time they are willing to hear or listen to anything about God is when they are either sick or in real trouble.

And yet to some others, God does indeed exist, and He listens to those who diligently seek and wait upon Him. And because of their strong belief in God, they have purposed in their lives to do the following:

1. Praise God daily for the gift of life and His goodness to them. They praise Him during the good times and the challenging/bad times.
2. They have learned to present their needs and wait for God's fullness of time. They believe that our God is always on time, and nothing takes Him by surprise.
3. They have set some time aside daily to read the good book and to go by its many promises.
4. Like Job, they have a purpose in their lives to trust in God no matter what. Does God hear or reward such ones? Yes indeed. In my next write-up entitled," the story of a woman taxi driver" I will share one moving story of how God intervenes in the lives of those who trust and wait upon Him.

Mahatma Gandhi Was Right

Mahatma Gandhi was right when he said," Saw me a Christian and I will become one."

I believe with all my heart that the most effective way to witness unto others about God/Jesus Christ is through practical Christianity. Yes, it's tough and yet to live the talk is the only thing that works. All other things are sure to fail. As taught by our Savior when on earth, His disciples need to be the light of the world. I would rather people look at me and say" indeed that person is a true follower of Jesus" than go around sending mixed messages. Just think of the following two examples/scenarios.

On a recent visit to Kenya, I witnessed/was involved in two situations/scenarios that made me think of Mahatma Gandhi's statement. One happened in Mombasa and another one in Nairobi.

As I was crossing from Likoni to the city on a ferry accompanied by my cousin, her husband preacher, and my wife, I was impressed and entertained by this young powerful preacher who moved from one side of the ferry to the other side preaching a powerful sermon that was supported by Scriptures and was well delivered. Later on, I found out that we were all touched. As a matter of fact, for a couple of days, we found ourselves talking about the sermon and more so the powerful young preacher. As you can tell, he had quite an impact and would have easily become a member of his club.

A couple of days later, we visited a place called Fort Jesus, just to see this historical place that witnessed the ugly face of the slave trade. It was while we were there reflecting on the past that we saw the young preacher for the second time. Just like that, we all found ourselves talking about the young preacher and his powerful message of repentance. He had become our hero. If only his parents knew how their son had touched 4 preachers so to speak!

But things were different this time around. We were disappointed or should I say I was. Even with my usual position of leaving Judgment to God alone and avoiding judging the book by its cover, his company of friends and their mannerism was not all that impressive. Even without going into any details, it was way below that which is expected of a preacher of his caliber. The two incidents were so contrary to each other. I would not reconcile the two.

Right there I was reminded of the importance to be careful and remember my people's saying "Getutu nkia maiso" (the forest has got the eyes." I felt so bad just to know that I too, have disappointed many in one way or the other. God, please forgive.

Away from Mombasa, a day before I left Nairobi, I made my way to a bank to collect money that was sent by a church member to help him buy some stuff from Nairobi. As I was filling the money gram withdrawal form, I happened to look through the glass at the cashier's desk and saw a religious booklet entitled," Health and Healing; April-June Sabbath School Bible Study Guide." On seeing that, I was impressed and expected better services. How come? That booklet is used by the SDA church and so on seeing that, I believed the owner must be a committed Christian. It's possible that He was, but his behavior, service, and customer service skills left a lot to be desired. Just judge by yourself.

He was more into talking on a cell phone than attending to me. It was as if I was not there. After I handed over the form, he took a long time flipping over my passport even before he had entered the information into the computer to see if I had money or not. When he opened his mouth to speak, he asked questions that were very annoying and had nothing to do with the money.

Am I complaining/whining? No! I am only trying to remind those of us who have decided to become Jesus' disciples and are embarked on promoting His kingdom to be careful lest we build and destroy at the same time. Yes, we are all human but telling people to "do that which we say and not do" has proved to be ineffective. If we have chosen this path, then let us follow the guidelines. Wherever we are and whatever we chose to do or say let us make sure that it confines with that which we profess to be. Anything less this has proved and will prove to be counter effective.

Even so good Lord, forgive us for where we have let you down and help us to become more like you. Amen.

A School Without Graduation

Ellen G White, my favorite author is very right when she writes that "marriage is a school without graduation." Come to think about it, all other schools have graduation but marriage. If they chose to talk/share, then those who are married will tell you that this is the one school that they have been tempted to quit several times. Except for the fact that the originator of this institution commanded all not to quit until death alone do them part, many would have left a long time ago. The person that they refer to as honey, darling, sweetheart, baby, the father/mother of my children from time to time gives them headache/hell. In what areas? It depends on one person to another. But if you are willing to listen and compare notes, then you might come up with something like this:

1. Disobedient: Some come to appoint when they chose not to listen, take orders or do anything.
2. Children issues: This is a whole forest that ranges from not having children to having one sex. Did I mention training them? Interestingly, each parent-father/ mother thinks that they are more expert in training the children than their partner. No one is willing to take second place or even to let things go. All want to be the headteacher and in many cases, teach all subjects. Talk about confusing the students/our children. One parent says one thing and another one says something else. Well, you know what you do in your home and therefore need no more lectures. I will leave it there.
3. Money and the woes that come with it. There is always fighting on the issue of money. Not enough money, how to spend it, whom to control it, how much to save. About pay slips, bank accounts and many others.

4. The challenges that come with in laws: Talk about in-laws (mother-in-law, father-in-law, brother-in-law, sister-in-law, and all other in-laws.) They come, invade, start giving rules and in the end up create confusion. Even those who have failed in their own homes try to make up in other people's homes. They seem to do well with the weak ones who always must take orders from elsewhere but their spouses.

None of these may be happening at your home. Good for you. But just in case you find yourself in a rocky/messy marriage or you know someone who does, then it might help to remember the following.

a. You had a greater say in choosing this your partner.
b. If you think that your wife/husband is the worst person that anyone can have, it might help to check around. You might be surprised to know that you have a good wife/husband without knowing.

Well, I do not claim to be an expert in this area just like I am not in many others. That said, you may want to try the following.

1. Know that there is no perfect marriage out there. Life is such that there will always be challenges. Stop taking things seriously or personally.
2. Spend more time changing yourself than your spouse. Many of us have a tendency of finding faults with our partners. Examine yourself daily to see if indeed you are not the troublemaker. Ask the Lord to change you first and then your spouse.
3. Avoid being suspicious and controlling. Accept to be guided by the golden rule as found in Mathew 7:12.

Just in case you have forgotten, remember that it takes three to keep the marriage going. Many have found out that things started getting off-hand the day they decided to leave God out of their daily system. God is the originator and founder of marriage is well equipped to fix any marital problems. Hire Him for free. Listen to Him, take notes, and learn daily how to be a good and acceptable husband/wife. Avoid entertaining the thoughts of quitting and instead work on your marriage until you succeed. Will you?

Understanding the Environment

Life as, full of headaches and people of all kinds of temperaments. Whether you like it or not, each day you will either find yourself in a not so friendly environment or you will come across people whose attitude and way of looking at things will be so different from your way. Since you are not likely to change anyone or anything for that matter, it might help to study and understand the environment in which you find yourself. That way you will adjust to fit in and in the end, save yourself from the daily uncalled-for drama. Take a look at the following scenarios and some suggestions.

1. If you join a school that subscribes itself to certain beliefs, you will do well to understand their beliefs, lifestyle, and philosophy. That way you can adjust to fit into that school instead of wasting a lot of time fighting it. If you don't like it, please find another school that will meet your needs or makes you happy.
2. If you decide/choose to be part of a certain people, tribes, race through marriage, do your best to see and do things the way they do and want it to be done. Avoid the temptation of trying to change them. It will most definitely backfire.
3. If you start working for an institution and soon or later find out that there is some boss/fellow workmate that you don't like for the way he/she sees and handles things, just learn quickly to adjust to the environment. Let your words be few. Whatever the boss says, just smile and do it. Your best bet is that with time you will get a different boss or better still you will join a different institution or run your own business/company.
4. If you join another congregation/church either as a pastor or parishioner, take your time and understand the

> culture of that church before you start saying or doing anything. Avoid the temptation of trying to impose your own changes. Even when you think that you know what's best, please try to slow down lest you end up frustrated.

Like I pointed out, life has never and will never be fair as long as we are in this part of the world. God's children are hard to understand and handle. Just leave them to their Father. Someone somewhere is going to try to give you hard time whether knowingly or unknowingly. While you may not change people you can choose to study, evaluate, and adjust basically to any environment. That way, you will have peace of mind and avoid the ulcers and headaches that unfortunately are the daily lot of the majority. Do you get my point?

You Can Do It!

Not that I am against them but rather disappointed with those individuals who have great talents but have either decided to be lazy or not that motivated to use them. Out there, are people with all kinds of talents; men who could do greater things if they chose to but for some reason, they are not doing anything.

Do you have a talent for writing? Why not put your thoughts/ideas on paper so that others can benefit from them? The best place to start is to learn from the experts and beginners in the field. Those of us who are at the very beginning know for sure that it will take time before the art is perfected. The thing about us is that we're willing to try.

Listen, if people like Pastor Birai, who have no command of the language can do it, why not you who are better placed? I challenge you to take that assignment seriously. Begin today. Once you are done, I promise to be the first one to buy your book.

Besides writing, there are people with talents in certain areas that they need to start using. The excuse that I often hear "I don't have time" does not hold water. I have learned in life that if anyone loves something, he or she will surely find the time. It's a question of convincing your mind to go for it. Once you have succeeded, please try to help encourage or mentor others. There is always a blessing that comes from giving it free. Try and let me know how it works for you.

I Am Not Worthy

On this Christmas day when many are thankful for the gift of Jesus Christ, and therefore are gathered in some place/church to sing and worship or around/under a table to eat and exchange gifts, my mind goes to those who at a given time in their lives expressed what many might regard as extreme humility.

It goes without saying that man by nature is arrogant and almost always wants to take credit or boast for talent or accomplishment in life. But there are those who have oftentimes felt like they have nothing to boast of and instead gave all the praise to God or those who showed them a favor. A few Biblical characters touched the core of my heart.

Mephibosheth

In deep appreciation of the friendship between them, king David one day decided to return a favor by doing something to the family of his once friend-Jonathan. Listen to him speak:

> *"When Mephibosheth son of Jonathan, the son of Saul, came to David, he bowed down to pay him honor. David said, "Mephibosheth!" At your service," he replied. "Don't be afraid," David said to him, "for I will surely show you kindness for the sake of your father Jonathan. I will restore to you all the land that belonged to your grandfather Saul and you will always eat at my table." (2 Samuel 9:6-7).*

Now, listen to how Mephibosheth answered," Mephibosheth bowed down and said, "What is your servant, that you should notice a dead dog like me?" Imagine that!

The Centurion

"And when Jesus was entered into Capernaum, there came unto him a centurion, beseeching him, And saying, Lord, my servant lies at home sick of the palsy, grievously tormented. And Jesus saith unto him, I will come and heal him. The centurion answered and said, Lord, I am not worthy that thou shouldest come under my roof: but speak the word only, and my servant shall be healed. For I am a man under authority, having soldiers under me: and I say to this man, Go, and he goes; and to another, Come, and he comes; and to my servant, Do this, and he does it. When Jesus heard it, he marveled, and said to them that followed, Verily I say unto you, I have not found so great faith, no, not in Israel. (Mathew 8:5-10)

The Phoenician Woman

"The woman came and knelt before him. "Lord, help me!" she said. He replied, "It is not right to take the children's bread and toss it to the dogs." "Yes it is, Lord," she said. "Even the dogs eat the crumbs that fall from their master's table." Then Jesus said to her, "Woman, you have great faith! Your request is granted." And her daughter was healed at that moment." (Mathew 15:25-28).

The Apostle Paul

"And so it was with me, brothers and sisters. When I came to you, I did not come with eloquence or human wisdom as I proclaimed to you the testimony about God. For I resolved to know nothing while I was with you except Jesus Christ and him crucified. I came to you in weakness with great fear

and trembling. My message and my preaching were not with wise and persuasive words, but with a demonstration of the Spirit's power, so that your faith might not rest on human wisdom, but on God's power. (1 Corinthians 2:1-5)

And so as I examine myself in the light of the cross and by comparing my faith, gratitude and accomplishments with that of the above, I find myself wanting in many ways. Therefore on this Christmas day, all I can say is that "Except for the Lord, I would not be here today". Lord Jesus, fame and riches I care not, but to serve you with great humility and faith that surpasses all that we have read above. Even so, help me please. Amen and thank you.

Jonathan and David: The Epitome of True Friendship

The story of Saul, his son, Jonathan, and David is a very interesting one to read. It not only opens our eyes and shows us what jealousy can do, but also shows us what true friendship means as demonstrated by David and Jonathan.

But before we get into their story, allow me to point out that as long as we can remember, we have always had friends; some who have stood with us in times of joy and in times of sorrow; others, influenced by other factors, have dropped us or deserted us at the time we needed them most. While Saul's jealousy drove him to want to kill an innocent David, the friendship between David and Jonathan revealed how unselfish both were. Here are the highlights:

1. Saul was the first King of Israel, chosen contrary to the will of God (1 Samuel 8:1-9).
2. Due to disobedience and impunity, God rejected Saul as a king (1 Samuel 16:1).
3. David, out there minding his own business as a shepherd, was chosen without campaigning to be the next king of Israel. As to why he was chosen, God said," The LORD does not look at the things people look at. People look at the outward appearance, but the LORD looks at the heart." (1 Samuel 6:7).
4. Moved by jealousy, Saul attempted several times to kill David, even though David had done nothing to deserve that (1 Samuel 18).
5. David had a chance to kill Saul but chose not to do so? Why? Listen to his touching reason,

"Then David went out of the cave and called out to Saul, "My lord the king!" When Saul looked behind him, David bowed down and prostrated himself with his face to the ground. He said to Saul, "Why do you listen when men say, 'David is bent on harming you'? This day you have seen with your own eyes how the LORD delivered you into my hands in the cave. Some urged me to kill you, but I spared you; I said, 'I will not lay my hand on my lord, because he is the Lord's anointed" (1 Samuel 24:8-10)

6. Beautiful. Lord, I hunger for this kind of attitude/resolve.

Even though Jonathan, the son of Saul, was the rightful candidate for the position of the next king of Israel, he relegated all that to his friend, David. (1 Samuel 18).

What about David? Did He love Jonathan? Yes indeed. Note the following:

1. On learning that Jonathan and his father Saul had died, David cried,

"Daughters of Israel, weep for Saul, who clothed you in scarlet and finery, who adorned your garments with ornaments of gold. How the mighty have fallen in battle! Jonathan lies slain on your heights. I grieve for you, Jonathan my brother; you were very dear to me. Your love for me was wonderful, more wonderful than that of women. "How the mighty have fallen! The weapons of war have perished!" (2 Samuel 1:24-27)

Wow!

2. Determined not to forget his dear friend, Jonathan, David did everything possible to reward his lame son-Mephibosheth. Here is what the Bible tells us:

"Jonathan son of Saul had a son who was lame in both feet. He was five years old when the news about Saul and Jonathan came from Jezreel. His nurse picked him up and fled, but as she hurried to leave, he fell and became disabled. His name was Mephibosheth." (2 Samuel 4:4)

"The king asked, "Is there no one still alive from the house of Saul to whom I can show God's kindness?" Ziba answered the king, "There is still a son of Jonathan; he is lame in both feet." "Where is he?" the king asked. Ziba answered, "He is at the house of Makir son of Ammiel in Lo Debar." So, King David, had him brought from Lo Debar from the house of Makir son of Ammiel. When Mephibosheth son of Jonathan, the son of Saul, came to David, he bowed down to pay him honor. David said, "Mephibosheth!" "At your service," he replied. "Don't be afraid," David said to him, "for I will surely show you kindness for the sake of your father Jonathan. I will restore to you all the land that belonged to your grandfather Saul, and you will always eat at my table." (2 Samuel 9:3-7)

Well, what else can I say; this friendship of Jonathan and David is the epitome of what friendship ought to be. Are you such a friend to your friends?

Let This Mind Be In You

As the year comes to an end, I continue to pray and do my part in emulating or having an attitude/mind like the following:

1. Be a peacemaker like Abraham

"So Abram said to Lot, "Let's not have any quarreling between you and me, or between your herders and mine, for we are close relatives. Is not the whole land before you? Let's part company. If you go to the left, I'll go to the right; if you go to the right, I'll go to the left." (Genesis 13:8-9)

2. Be meek/humble like Moses

"Now the man Moses was very meek, more than all people who were on the face of the earth" (Numbers 12:3).

3. Give God credit as Daniel did.

"Then Daniel went to Arioch, whom the king had appointed to execute the wise men of Babylon, and said to him, "Do not execute the wise men of Babylon. Take me to the king, and I will interpret his dream for him." Arioch took Daniel to the king at once and said, "I have found a man among the exiles from Judah who can tell the king what his dream means. "The king asked Daniel (also called Belteshazzar), "Are you able to tell me what I saw in my dream and interpret it?" Daniel replied, "No wise man, enchanter, magician or diviner can explain to the king the mystery he has asked about, but there is a God in heaven who reveals mysteries. He has shown King Nebuchadnezzar what will happen in days to come. Your dream and the visions that passed through your mind as you were lying in bed are

these: "As Your Majesty was lying there, your mind turned to things to come, and the revealer of mysteries showed you what is going to happen. As for me, this mystery has been revealed to me, not because I have greater wisdom than anyone else alive, but so that Your Majesty may know the interpretation and that you may understand what went through your mind." (Daniel 2:24-30).

1. Be willing to decrease like John, the Baptist

"He must become greater; I must become less" (John 3:30).

2. . Be generous like Cornelius:

"At Caesarea, there was a man named Cornelius, a centurion in what was known as the Italian Regiment. He and all his family were devout and God-fearing; he gave generously to those in need and prayed to God regularly." (Acts 10:1-2).

3. Be an encourager like Joseph:

"Joseph, a Levite from Cyprus, whom the apostles called Barnabas (which means "son of encouragement"), sold a field he owned and brought the money and put it at the apostles' feet." (Acts 4:36-37)

4. Have the mind of Jesus

"In your relationships with one another, has the same mindset as Christ Jesus"

Who, being in very nature God?

Lord Jesus, I know that I am far from being like any of the above, but I am working on it. I need your help every hour to be where you want me to be. Help me, dear Lord. Amen.

What Shall I Render Unto The Lord?

God has indeed been so good to us. At a given time in our journey home, the Lord has intervened and changed our sorrow into joy. Many throughout the centuries have reacted in a different way towards God's abundant blessings. The following have always inspired me:

David

David was picked as a little shepherd boy to be the king of Israel. He attracted many enemies including his son Absalom who attempted an unsuccessful coup to enthrone his father. David himself committed the crime of killing Urriah and taking his wife. Despite all these setbacks, God did not leave him alone. His testimony testified to that. Here it's:

> *What shall I render to the LORD for all his benefits to me? I will lift the cup of salvation and call on the name of the LORD, I will pay my vows to the LORD in the presence of all his people (Psalms 116:12).*

Daniel

During the night the mystery was revealed to Daniel in a vision. Then Daniel praised the God of heaven and said:

> *Praise be to the name of God forever and ever; wisdom and power are his. He changes times and seasons; he deposes kings and raises others. He gives wisdom to the wise and knowledge to the discerning. He reveals deep and hidden things; he knows what lies in darkness, and light dwells with him. I thank and praise you, God of my ancestors:*

You have given me wisdom and power, you have made known to me what we asked of you, you have made known to us the dream of the king." (Daniel 2:19-23)

Hannah, the mother of Samuel

"I prayed for this child, and the LORD has granted me what I asked of him. So now I give him to the LORD. For his whole life, he will be given over to the LORD." And he worshiped the LORD there." (1 Samuel 1:27-28).

Simeon

Simeon, a servant of God was so delighted that God fulfilled a promise of letting him see the Messiah. He was ready to die after that. Listen to him:

"Simeon took him in his arms and praised God, saying: "Sovereign Lord, as you have promised, you may now dismiss your servant in peace. For my eyes have seen your salvation," (Luke 2:28-30).

Mary Magdalene

Jesus meant everything to Mary Magdalene. Note the following:

1. He casts demons out of her 7 times (Mark 16:9).
2. Jesus sets her free from being stoned (John 8:1-11).
3. Jesus resurrected his brother, Lazarus (John 11).

In deep appreciation for all that and more, she worked and saved all her salary for the whole year. She used all her savings to purchase very expensive perfume. Here is how she used that perfume.

"A woman in that town who lived a sinful life learned that Jesus was eating at the Pharisee's house, so she came there with an alabaster jar of perfume. As she stood behind him at his feet weeping, she began to wet his feet with her tears. Then she wiped them with her hair, kissed them and poured perfume on them." (Luke 7:37-38).

A leper

One leper on realizing that he had been cured of the dreadful disease of leprosy went back praising God. Here is part of the story:

"One of them, when he saw he was healed, came back, praising God in a loud voice. He threw himself at Jesus' feet and thanked him—and he was a Samaritan" (Luke 17:15-16).

What's your story? What does Jesus mean to you?

People Whom We Should Avoid

As children, we were made to understand that there were kids on the block or in the village that we would play with, eat at their home, invite to our home and there were those that we were not supposed to. The same information has been passed over to us repeatedly.

As if reading from the same script our parents, teachers, spouses, pastors and employers have at sundry times reminded us to avoid among many, people who:

1. Will lead us into sin.
2. Will mislead us by encouraging us to quit school/a jobs, run away from home, our parents and/or abandon our families.
3. Have a bad reputation or a bad history

Does the Bible say anything as regards this issue? Interestingly it does and backs the same notion: Look at the following passages:

"Blessed is the one who does not walk in step with the wicked or stand in the way that sinners take or sit in the company of mockers, but whose delight is in the law of the LORD, and who meditates on his law day and night" (Psalms 1:1-2).

"My son, if sinners entice you, do not give in to them" (Proverbs 1:10).

"A violent man entices his neighbor and leads him down a path that is not good." (Proverbs 16:29).

"Do not be misled: "Bad company corrupts good character." (1 Corinthians 15:33).

"In the name of the Lord Jesus Christ, we command you, brothers, to keep away from every brother who is idle and does not live according to the teaching you received from us." (In the name of the Lord Jesus Christ, we command you, brothers, to keep away from every brother who is idle and does not live according to the teaching you received from us. (2 Thessalonians 3:6)

So, let us choose our friends, and choose them with wisdom.

Behold I Come Quickly

If you are a keen Bible student, then I think you have noticed that out there are many signs that point to the soon return of our Lord and Savior, Jesus Christ. In my devotion this morning (3:00 AM) through the book of Revelation, I was touched by Revelation 3:11, "Behold, I come quickly: hold that fast, which thou hast, that no man takes thy crown."

From the time when Jesus Himself gave the promise of His second coming," Do not let your hearts be troubled. You believe in God; believe also in me. My Father's house has many rooms; if that were not so, would I have told you that I am going there to prepare a place for you? And if I go and prepare a place for you, I will come back and take you to be with me that you also may be where I am. You know the way to the place where I am going." (John 14:1-4), many have patiently waited for the fulfillment of this promise.

While many have gone into their graves without having witnessed the fulfillment of this promise, and some of the living followers have or are at the point of giving up, the truth of the matter is that He will surely return. Peter believes that the problem is more on us as opposed to Jesus. He writes, "The Lord is not slow in keeping his promise, as some understand slowness. Instead he is patient with you, not wanting anyone to perish, but everyone to come to repentance." (2 Peter 3:9)

I guess my question for all of us is this" Are we ready?" When we examine ourselves in the light of the sure word of God, are we ready to welcome Him at His second appearance?

Lord Jesus, more and more I realize that it won't be long before you return to take your children home, I fast daily and pray that I will be among those who will be saved. Forgive me where I have sinned against you and wronged fellow human beings.

Running Away From God

Running is a good thing. How so?

1. Some people run as a way of doing exercise that our bodies need.
2. Some have made a career out of running.
3. We all run away from danger. At such times we pray and hope that our legs will carry us as faster as possible.

The thing that we don't want to do, is to run away from God. You mean that there are people who do that. Yes indeed. Influenced by the things of this world, many have for years tried to run away from God. Things like what? They include the following:

- Money
- Career
- Fame/talent
- Education
- Deceptive lifestyle and freedom
- Marriage
- Good looking

Some of us were at one time God-fearing individuals. Some of us were even brought up in families where the fear/respect of/for God was the way of life. But when our status changed, we decided to have nothing to do with God. Listen to me, all the above are only temporal. They come and go.

Just take a few minutes and reflect on your life thus far. Hasn't God contributed in some way to your success? So what wrong thing did you find in Him? For how long will you run away from Him? Why do you always try to come up with all kinds of excuses to defend your view of life?

My friend, turn around and run back to God. Forget about defending yourself. Waste no time for you and I are living on a borrowed life, which can come to an end at any time. Jesus is calling you to open the door of your heart.

> *"He pleads, "I know your deeds, that you are neither cold nor hot. I wish you were either one or the other! So, because you are lukewarm—neither hot nor cold—I am about to spit you out of my mouth. You say, 'I am rich; I have acquired wealth and do not need a thing.' But you do not realize that you are wretched, pitiful, poor, blind and naked. I counsel you to buy from me gold refined in the fire, so you can become rich, and white clothes to wear, so you can cover your shameful nakedness, and salve to put on your eyes, so you can see.*
>
> *Those whom I love I rebuke and discipline. So be earnest and repent. Here I am! I stand at the door and knock. If anyone hears my voice and opens the door, I will come in and eat with that person, and they with me." (Revelation 3:20).*

A Bitter Cry for The Wayward Ones

In history, some have been badly hurt; hurt because those that they loved and cared for (parents, children, spouses, church members and friends) chose to travel on a route that either immediately or with time will turn around and destroy them. These individuals have not only pleaded with their loved ones to change course but have pleaded with the good Lord to intervene in the lives of their loved ones. Some have spent or lost lots of money as they struggled to bail out their loved ones. In going through the Bible, I have found some examples that have really touched me. I would like to share those with you.

Moses

Not that Moses applied for the job, but that God chose him to lead the children of Israel from Egypt to the Promised Land. This was in response to their cry to God reminding Him of the promises that He had made to Abraham (Exodus 2). Enroute; they not only whined but also blamed God and Moses for taking them out of Egypt. There are times that they wanted to go back to Egypt where they ate meat and had a good time. Several times, God wanted to wipe them out, but the man Moses interceded for them. Read on:

> *"And the LORD said unto Moses, I have seen these people, and behold, it is a stiff-necked people"*
>
> *Now, therefore, let me alone, that my wrath may wax hot against them, and that I may consume them: and I will make of thee a great nation. And Moses besought the LORD his God, and said, LORD, why doth thy wrath wax hot against thy people, which thou hast brought forth out of the land of Egypt with great power, and with a mighty hand?*

Wherefore should the Egyptians speak, and say, for mischief did he bring them out, to slay them in the mountains, and to consume them from the face of the earth? Turn from thy fierce wrath and repent of this evil against thy people. Remember Abraham, Isaac, and Israel, thy servants, to whom you swore by your own self, and said unto them, I will multiply your seed as the stars of heaven, and all this land that I have spoken of will I give unto your seed, and they shall inherit it forever. And the LORD repented of the evil which he thought to do unto his people." (Exodus 32:9-14)

Wow! This is powerful! What else can I say?

David

David loved his son Absalom even when the wayward young man staged a coup to remove his father from his throne. Listen to how David cried on receiving the news that the young man Absalom had died: Incredible love for a wayward son.

"The king asked the Cushite, "Is the young man Absalom safe?"

The Cushite replied, "May the enemies of my lord the king and all who rise to harm you be like that young man." The king was shaken. He went up to the room over the gateway and wept. As he went, he said: "O my son Absalom! My son, my son Absalom! If only I had died instead of you—O Absalom, my son, my son! (1 Samuel 18:32-33).

Paul

The apostle Paul was ready and willing to be cursed out if only that would save his people-the people of Israel:

> *"I speak the truth in Christ—I am not lying, my conscience confirms it through the Holy Spirit— I have great sorrow and unceasing anguish in my heart. For I could wish that I were cursed and cut off from Christ for the sake of my people, those of my own race" (Romans 9:1-3).*

Jesus

His cry over Jerusalem, the city He loved is His cry for us today. Oh yes, I can hear it loud and clear. Lord, I am sorry for the way we have treated you!

> *"O Jerusalem, Jerusalem, thou that kills the prophets, and stones them which are sent unto thee, how often I would have gathered thy children together, even as a hen gathered her chickens under her wings, and ye would not! Behold, your house is left unto you desolate. For I say unto you, Ye shall not see me henceforth, till ye shall say, Blessed, is he that cometh in the name of the Lord." (Matthew 23:37-39).*

What about today

I hear the cry of many parents, children, siblings, and/or couples over their loved ones. They cry day in and day out for God to turn their sorrow into joy. Many parents have gone into their graves while praying for their children and hoping to see a miracle.

Well, even so, come to Lord Jesus. Amen and thank you so much!

Jesus and the Needy Ones

While on earth, Jesus not only Preached, taught, and healed all kinds of diseases (Mathew 4:23), but also took care of the physical needs of the majority poor. Repeatedly, the Bible records that moved by compassion, Jesus took an action by meeting the needs of the crowd that followed Him. It's recorded that He identified Himself with those who were being mistreated/harassed and did everything possible to make their life on earth more bearable. The following passages bear testimony to that:

1. Moved by compassion, He fed the five thousand, besides women and children, (Mathew 14:13-21).
2. Moved by compassion, He fed the four thousand who had not eaten for 3 straight days (Matthew 15:29-39).
3. When he saw the crowds, he had compassion on them, because they were harassed and helpless, like sheep without a shepherd. Then he said to his disciples, "The harvest is plentiful, but the workers are few. Ask the Lord of the harvest, therefore, to send out workers into his harvest field "(Mathew 9:35-38).
4. "And there came a leper to him, beseeching him, and kneeling to him, and saying unto him, If thou wilt, thou canst make me clean.
5. And Jesus, moved with compassion, put forth his hand, and touched him, and saith unto him, I will; be thou clean." Mark 1:40-41).
6. "Moved with compassion, Jesus touched their eyes; and immediately they regained their sight and followed Him." (Mathew 20:34).

Jesus expects us (His followers) to do the same towards our fellow human beings. Before returning to heaven, He left His disciples with a new commandment, "to love one another as He had loved them" (John 13:34-35). The Bible records and appreciates the efforts of those who were involved in the acts of assisting others. Two of such were Tabitha (Acts 9:36-42) and Cornelius (Acts 10)

James even goes to an extent of associating true religion with the helping of others. He wrote," Religion that God our Father accepts as pure and faultless is this: to look after orphans and widows in their distress and to keep oneself from being polluted by the world." (James 1:27).

Is it any wonder that Judgment will be partly based on how we responded to the many needs of God's children? Yes indeed, those who were naked, destitute of daily needs, in prison and many others. Read the entire account on Mathew 25:31-46). In this passage, Jesus identifies Himself with those that the community considered an outcast and didn't have time for them.

Let us be careful how we relate with those who seem to have nothing to pay back. Jesus expects us to be moved with compassion and give them hope to continue to live. Let us make a little heaven for such ones here and now.

Even so heavenly father, use me to meet the needs of the majority poor, even if it means just one dear Lord. Bless me so that I can bless your children. Lord, I am willing to give it all. You know that I mean it, dear Lord. Amen

Whenever Bad Things Happen To Us

There are at least three ways of interpreting the bad/unfortunate things that happen to us on the daily basis:

1. Bad things happen to us because of our bad choices. Many have gotten into serious trouble/problems due to choosing the wrong friends/company, a destructive lifestyle, marrying the wrong person or eating/ drinking the wrong stuff. In such cases, we are to blame for our own choices. Note what the following passages say:

"This day I call heaven and earth as witnesses against you that I have set before you life and death, blessings and curses. Now choose life, so that you and your children may live" (Deuteronomy 30:19).

"Enter through the narrow gate. For wide is the gate and broad is the road that leads to destruction, and many enter through it. But small is the gate and narrow the road that leads to life, and only a few find" (Matthew 7:13-14).

2. There are other times that the good Lord allows disappointment to come our way. This is so especially when He wants to accomplish His mission in our lives. He left John the Baptist to die in prison, to become a source of encouragement to those who might be called to travel the same route. Remember the story of Job? God had a point that He wanted to make. Job stood firm and thus defeated the devil.

"I have told you these things, so that in me you may have peace. In this world you will have trouble. But take heart! I have overcome the world." (John 16:33)

If you suffer, it should not be as a murderer or thief or any other kind of criminal, or even as a meddler. However, if you suffer as a Christian, do not be ashamed, but praise God that you bear that name. For it is time for judgment to begin with the family of God; and if it begins with us, what will the outcome be for those who do not obey the gospel of God? And "If it is hard for the righteous to be saved, what will become of the ungodly and the sinner?" So then, those who suffer according to God's will commit themselves to their faithful Creator and continue to do well." (1 Peter 4:15-19)

"Precious in the sight of the LORD is the death of his saints." (Psalms 116:15)

"As he went along, he saw a man blind from birth. His disciples asked him, "Rabbi, who sinned, this man or his parents, that he was born blind?"

"Neither this man nor his parents sinned," said Jesus, "but this happened so that the works of God might be displayed in him. As long as it is the day, we must do the works of him who sent me. The night is coming when no one can work. While I am in the world, I am the light of the world." (John 9:1-5)

"Therefore, in order to keep me from becoming conceited, I was given a thorn in my flesh, a messenger of Satan, to torment me. Three times I pleaded with the Lord to take it away from me. But he said to me, "My grace is sufficient for you, for my power is made perfect in weakness." Therefore, I will boast all the more gladly about my weaknesses, so

that Christ's power may rest on me. That is why, for Christ's sake, I delight in weaknesses, in insults, in hardships, in persecutions, in difficulties. For when I am weak, then I am strong." (2 Corinthians 12:7-10).

3. And thirdly, bad things happen to us because of sin.

To the woman, he said, "I will make your pains in childbearing very severe; with painful labor, you will give birth to children. Your desire will be for your husband, and he will rule over you." To Adam, he said, "Because you listened to your wife and ate fruit from the tree about which I commanded you, 'You must not eat from it,'" Cursed is the ground because of you; through painful toil, you will eat food from it all the days of your life. It will produce thorns and thistles for you, and you will eat the plants of the field. By the sweat of your brow, you will eat your food until you return to the ground since from it you were taken; for dust you are and to dust, you will return." (Genesis 3:16-19)

"For the wages of sin is death, but the gift of God is eternal life in Christ Jesus our Lord." (Romans 6:23)

"Therefore, just as sin entered the world through one man, and death through sin, and in this way death came to all people because all sinned—" (Romans 5:12)

So, any time anything bad/unfortunate happens to us, try to view it through at least the above three. There would be other reasons, but my search has settled on the above three.

Every Day Is Different

No two days are the same in every aspect. Instead, every day is quite unique and different in many ways. Some days begin very well and end up with a string of challenges here and there. Other days begin with so many disturbing challenges but end up with exciting news.

If you talk to many people, they will tell you that it seems like in each day, there are more disappointments than what many may term as good news. I am sure that many of us can handle good days or days with good news such as getting a job, finding a life partner, passing an examination, getting promoted, receiving complete healing, buying a house/car and such.

But what about handling or dealing with the day that comes with bad news such as losing a job, being dumped by a wife/husband or one that you were hoping that he/she would be your future partner, accidents, death of a loved one, sickness and such like? You and I can pretty well handle any day depending on how much we trust and count on our God's so many promises. Depends really on how well we are anchored in God. The question is, will your anchor hold? Here are the many promises that we can count on during tough times.

"For I know the plans I have for you," declares the LORD, "plans to prosper you and not to harm you, plans to give you hope and a future." (Jeremiah 29:11).

"Yet Jerusalem says, "The LORD has deserted us; the Lord has forgotten us."

"Never! Can a mother forget her nursing child? Can she feel no love for the child she has borne? But even if that were possible, I would not forget you!" (Isaiah 49:14-15)

"And we know that in all things God works for the good of those who love him, who have been called according to His purposes" (Romans 8:28).

"Because of the Lord's great love, we are not consumed, for his compassions never fail. They are new every morning; great is your faithfulness." (Lamentations 3:22-23).

"The LORD is my shepherd, I lack nothing. He makes me lie down in green pastures, he leads me beside quiet waters, and he refreshes my soul. He guides me along the right paths for his name's sake. Even though I walk through the darkest valley, I will fear no evil, for you are with me; your rod and your staff, they comfort me.

You prepare a table before me in the presence of my enemies. You anoint my head with oil; my cup overflows. Surely your goodness and love will follow me all the days of my life, and I will dwell in the house of the LORD forever." (Psalms 23:1-6)

With the preceding assurances, those who trust in the Lord can face any day with confidence that the good Lord will see them through any storm.

Even so, Lord Jesus, help us to trust in you always, no matter how the day begins and ends.

Living With Others

We came to this world alone at birth and will sure go alone at death. All the other time, we have no choice but to deal with fellow human beings. Really? Here, look:

1. We'll begin life by living with parents, siblings, nannies' relatives, and neighbors.
2. As we grow, we'll mix with others at school (primary, high school, college, university) and church.
3. When we start working, we'll either travel to find a job or get one near us whereby we'll have to deal with others.
4. When we become of age and get married, we'll sure deal with others, some of whom we might have not met before.

So, as you can see, we'll always deal with other people besides ourselves. No wonder the Bible tells us to learn how to live peacefully with others. "If it is possible, as far as it depends on you, live at peace with everyone." (Romans 12:18). "If possible" goes to show that living with others is not all that easy. One must let go of many things for him or her to live peacefully with others. Note the following facts:

"Make every effort to live in peace with everyone and to be holy; without holiness, no one will see the Lord." (Hebrews 12:14).

"Strive not with a man without cause, if he has done thee no harm." (Proverbs 3:30).

"Salt is good, but if it loses its saltiness, how can you make it salty again? Have salt among yourselves and be at peace with each other" (Mark 9:50).

"So, Abram said to Lot, "Let's not have any quarreling between you and me, or between your herders and mine, for we are close relatives" (Genesis 13:8).

So, to live with others, one must do among other things the following:

1. Purpose in your heart to let many things go.
2. Strive to become a peacemaker as opposed to a troublemaking
3. Be willing to decrease for others to increase.
4. Choose humility as a way of life.
5. Let go of revenge, anger, arrogance, and despising others.
6. Always practice the golden rule (Matthew 7:12).
7. Work on changing oneself first instead of spending all time trying to change others.
8. Let us learn to always avoid gossip.

Once we realize that we need others in our lives, yes, even the untouchables, we'll go the extra mile in accommodating all. On our own, we cannot but with Jesus on our side, all things are possible. Let us embark on that effort.

A Small Crack on My Car Window Screen

I can't tell you how it got there for I don't know. All I know is that a while ago, I noticed this small crack on my front car window screen; so small that there was no need to worry. I told myself not to worry as in due time the situation will be taken care of. And I am almost certain that you know the rest of the story. I didn't get to do it as planned.

Yesterday morning, I was shocked to find out that the small crack has now moved from its location and in fact affected the whole window screen. It's going to cost more to fix it, all because of my failure to act immediately. You know that I regret my slow base of not taking care of the problem when it was minute. With great regrets, I was reflecting on this car issue when it occurred to me that some of the things that end up getting people into trouble started small or little here and there. Here, looks at this:

1. Pathological liars started by telling just one small lie.
2. Abusing drugs started as a way of just tasting.
3. Stealing started by maybe stealing food in the house.
4. Those who finally quit reading the Bible or attending the weekly church meetings start by skipping one week, then a month and then they disappear not to be found.

Many parents know for a fact that they in away contributed to the spoiling of their kids. They spoiled them by providing anything they wanted. We then allowed them to mix with other kids, to sleep over, to go to movies and name it. By the time we come to realize, these kids are way too far that we cannot help them. Instruct, rebuke with kindness, reason out with them but don't allow them to wander like sheep without a shepherd.

Equally important, avoid the temptation of inviting temptation unto you by cheating yourself that you are strong enough to overcome. Let us pay attention to those things that we regard as small for, with time, they turn around and hurt us.

A Daily Reminder to Myself

During my many years of struggling with sickness, poverty and sending myself to school, I prayed and promised God and my parents' certain things. Like what?

1. I pleaded with God to help me attain the highest education possible and yet help me to remain humble always. Over the years I have prayed that no traces of arrogance/pride should be noticed in my daily life.
2. I promised God that I will always be there for His needy children regardless of race, tribe, gender, status, and age. I'll always sacrifice to assist those who need my help.
3. I promised God that I will serve Him at whatever cost. I know that I have let Him down repeatedly, but I do remind myself daily of that promise.
4. Not willing that any of my siblings should go through what I went through, I promised my parents that I will do my best to help each of my siblings to realize their dream in life

Every single day, I remind myself of those promises and the need to keep them through.

How about you? Are there any promises that perhaps you made to your God, parents, siblings, spouse, and children? Ever taken time to reflect on the progress of those promises? Is it possible that having realized your goal in life, you have forgotten any or all of them?

Even so, help me heavenly father so as not to forget any one of the promises.

My Greatest Investment

Today, I received a letter from my younger brother that made me shed tears of joy. It was about my nephew's colorful graduation from Maseno University, Kenya. It was yet another miracle and one more down. How do you mean?

I am not a millionaire or anything for that matter. Many people if asked, will point to this all that investment that they have managed to do in their lifetime. I do not have anything to show; this even though I received my first salary in July 1978. How come?

Unwilling to see my siblings suffer the same way I did, I purposed in my heart when I started working to invest in their welfare. I decided to invest in their education to see their dream come true. Since then, I and later my wife and I have invested much of our resources to assist those who were willing to go to school. This has passed on to nephews, nieces, in laws, their children and others.

The story of my nephew who just graduated is a very touching one. His late mother (my youngest sister) a teacher by profession, died at 38 years old and left behind a jobless husband and 3 boys. Several years later, their father passed away. My wife and I stepped in to send him to high school and then Maseno University (parallel program.) His has been perhaps the most expensive. But now he is done and got himself a job for which we are truly thankful.

I share this with the sole purpose of encouraging those who have undertaken the same project. Out there are many who have for years sacrificed to help someone go to school. I know that you have denied yourself basic needs to assist here and there. Some of those that you are helping are sure to disappoint if they have not done that already. But from time to time, there is a success story, a reason to celebrate and give glory to God.

Yes, you may not belong to the club of the rich and famous, but in heaven, God will have your name included in the list of those who sacrificed to help His needy children, and to you, the Lord will say," Well done; come thou blessed of my father for I was in need and you.....(Mathew 25:31..).

And remember," let us not be weary in well doing for in due season we shall reap, if we faint not"(Galatians 6:9).

Thank you, Jesus, thank you. And thank y'all who have sacrificed to help others.

My Life as a Preacher

I have come a long way. I have never understood why the Lord of the universe called unwilling sinners like me to the gospel ministry. Let me walk you through my life as a minister.

My late father was a very hard-working man. Born and brought up in a very poor family, he worked his way up to become a very successful businessman. He was a man of faith and greatly loved His God and gave generously to all who were in need. Our home was like a school or camp place for many years. My father planted the SDA Church in our village. Later on, he gave up his faith and married four wives. He lived to be 108 years old. He died a very committed SDA believer. My late mother was born and brought up catholic. She converted into SDA and served as a deaconess and church treasurer for many years. Both of my late parents loved God and prayed for their children daily. I cherish and truly miss their prayers. When I was young, I stole, brew and drank alcohol and smoked cigarettes. Some days I would walk into a church a complete drunkard. I do not even know how I became an Adventist. I must have been influenced by my older sisters.

For reasons I have never understood, my mother suffered greatly as she lost her 7 children at various ages to who knows what. Due to this, I left my home when I was in fourth grade and lived with all kinds of relatives for most of my life.It was during this time that I was baptized and became so dedicated. I read the Bible and spiritual books by Ellen G White in great humility and went from village to village preaching. I had no desire for the things of this world. Then, I preached and called sin by its right name. I did not spare the sinners. That has all changed and still working on it.

Every school that I went to, I started the SDA group and was their leader. Many called me their pastor. I was a very staunch SDA and a very strict vegetarian. Nothing or no one would convince me to work on Sabbath. No, not even my parents or any other person. After high school, my local pastor talked me into joining the pastoral ministry, something that I refused without a second thought. It took 6 years before accepting the call. After that, it took me 13 years in college/university preparing for pastoral ministry. I joined the ministry in 1986.

Here is what I have learned as a minister:

1. Like Paul, I feel like I am the chief of sinners.
2. Pastoral work is very challenging; it's not all that easier as many think.
3. For a pastor to succeed, daily Bible study, prayer, faith, humility and complete surrender are a must.
4. A pastor must be in tune with heaven all the time.
5. A pastor must love his/her members and be there for them 24x7.
6. A pastor must avoid any influence of evil, practicing partiality/favoritism, going for revenge, and putting too much emphasis on money.
7. A pastor must learn to delegate and teach by example.
8. A pastor must be widely read and understand current affairs.
9. In preaching to others, a pastor needs to remember that he is a sinner too and therefore from time to time take a leave from the pulpit and be at the receiving end.
10. A pastor must choose humility, apply listening skills, read widely on administration/leadership and be careful in his way of presentation.

As you can tell, we the preachers are daily learning from the master. We are not there yet but are surely working on it. Bear with us as we learn of the science and art of ministry.

A Careless Way of Doing Things

How I wish that some of us can be careful about how we do things. Many things have gone wrong due to the careless way of doing things. How so?

1. Driving through Minnesota roads, you cannot help but see so many cars in a ditch. What is sad is that some of these cars are there due to a careless way of driving by some motorists. Even with bad weather and the knowledge of what careless driving can do, certain motorists just can't get it. The driveway passed the posted speed, passed by other motorists and ignore the traffic lights thus putting their own lives and that of others at risk.
2. A lot of students fail their exams and term papers because of their careless way of answering questions or due to their failure to pay attention to the fine details.
3. Some have lost their jobs/licenses because of being careless in handling certain aspects of their work. Have you heard of med error? Some nurses and those passing medications have been in trouble for this. Certain jobs call for extra carefulness.
4. Some people are just too careless when it comes to what comes out of their mouths. They just say anything that comes out of their mouths. In essence, they speak and then think. Others have been in trouble for their careless manner of addressing their bosses.
5. Perhaps the most careless of all, is the carelessness that many depict with the issue of our salvation. Simply put, many just don't care. This even though it took Jesus to descend to this planet earth, born in a manger, lived among us and was crucified as a criminal so as to save

> us. Surely, how can anyone be so careless with such love and ultimate sacrifice? Despite our careless attitude, Jesus still loves us and wants us to be saved.

Friends and family, in all that we do, let us do all it takes to avoid being careless

A Good Name

Concerning a good name, the Bible has the following to say:

A good name is more desirable than great riches; to be esteemed is better than silver or gold." (Proverbs 22:1)

"A good name is better than fine perfume," (Ecclesiastes 7:1).

A good name has to do with who we are (eat, drink, dress, reason, think, react to situations); how we treat others; how we care about others, and the motives behind all that we do. Any time anyone's name is mentioned, people attach all these things before they come up with their own verdict of what they think of such a person. May be Maybe a liar, a thief, arrogant, boastful, always taking advantage of others, undermines others, thinks of himself/herself always, a drunkard, a trouble maker, mean, jealousy person, pretender, lives double standard and....

A good name will take you anywhere and will live on many years after you have passed away. Such a name will benefit some of those associated with you. What people think of a person usually comes out when the community is dealing with certain issues, one moves from one place to another, a leader leaves office, or one passes away. That is when people pour out what was in their hearts. If a person is or was considered a good person, then some parents like to name their children after such a person.

The Bible presents certain individuals that were regarded as good people (having a good name) "In Joppa, there was a disciple named Tabitha (in Greek her name is Dorcas); she was always doing good and helping the poor. About that time she became sick and died, and her body was washed and placed in an upstairs room. Lydda was near Joppa; so when the disciples heard that

Peter was in Lydda, they sent two men to him and urged him, "Please come at once!"

Peter went with them, and when he arrived he was taken upstairs to the room. All the widows stood around him, crying and showing him the robes and other clothing that Dorcas had made while she was still with them." (Acts 9:36-39).

Joseph, a Levite from Cyprus, whom the apostles called Barnabas (which means "son of encouragement" (Acts 4:23).

What kind of a person are you? How do others (spouse, parents, children, siblings, friends, workmates, schoolmates, the community, your church members, your pastor, and fellow church members) think about you? If you relocate or die like all of us will someday, will anyone miss you or will they be happy that you are gone?

And finally, what does God think about us? What is His evaluation of you?

Lord Jesus, please help us to live a life that pleases you. Use us for your own honor and glory. May wc continually think of how we can help others and avoid the temptation of always thinking about ourselves? May we learn to esteem others more than us.

Free To Commit Sin

There is no question that we live in a free world. Each one of us is free to do anything that we want without anyone saying anything, yea even to sin. We are free to commit either private or public sin, and not only rejoice but also defend it with or without employing a lawyer or asking for forgiveness. What do you mean by private or public sin? Which one is wicked?

Well, since you asked to allow me to clarify. Private sin is the kind of sin that you commit and probably no one knows except you and the person that you committed with and of course God. On the other hand, public sin is that sin that you commit with arrogance, stubbornness, it's known to all, and yet you defend it without any sense of remorse. Which sin is more serious? While sin is sin and there is no difference, in my opinion, the latter -public sin-has greater effects, more so if it's committed by those who know that it's wrong to do such. How so?

1. Public sin has and can destroy the entire congregation just like that.
2. Public sin encourages and empowers others to commit the same if not worse.
3. Public sin glorifies the devil and humiliates the Lord of the universe.
4. Public sin gives others a license to commit sin.
5. God has often time punished such very severely

Look at the following:

1. When Sodom and Gomorrah chose immorality as a way of life, God destroyed the Twin Cities -Genesis 19.
2. When a man decided to pick sticks on the Sabbath, God ordered such to be killed Numbers 24.

3. When Miriam and Aaron opposed Moses openly, Miriam came down with leprosy immediately-Numbers 12.
4. When Korah and his friends resulted in an open rebellion, the land opened and they were swallowed alive.
5. When King Belshazzar decided to misuse the Holy items, God killed him the same night-Daniel 5.
6. Ananias and his wife died in their attempt to deceive the Holy ghost-Acts 5.
7. King Herode was killed instantly for failing to give God glory. -Acts 12

There is no question that our God is kind, loving, forgiving and long suffering. But a read through the Bible reveals that God abhors sins that are committed openly without any remorse whatsoever. In such cases, God is known to have acted shifty and without mercy.

You and I need to remember that God is not a human being to play around with. If we have formed a habit of committing sin and defending it openly, let us be very careful. Let us tread carefully lest we learn in a hard way.

Even so dear Lord, forgive us for our recklessness, stupidity and carelessness. Forgive us for we have misled many by our open and shameful sins. Yes, forgive us even for that which we regard as private sin for all things are manifest before you. Amen

The Impending Persecution

The Bible not only speaks of the past persecution that many of the faithful ones throughout the centuries have gone through but also the last and perhaps the most severe one that awaits God's elect. When Jesus was on earth, He spoke so often about it but assured His faithful ones not to worry as He will take care of them. The one thing that He urged them is to pray that such doesn't happen in winter and or on Sabbath. Let us pull out some of what Jesus said:

> *Two things that we need to remember is that some of what Jesus said is known as dual prophecy; it happened during the time proceeding the fall of Jerusalem/destruction of the temple and that it will happen again. Another point that Jesus made it clear is that whoever endures to the end, the same will be saved. Note that He cautioned His followers not even to worry about defending themselves because He will take care of that.*
>
> *"Then you will be handed over to be persecuted and put to death, and you will be hated by all nations because of me. At that time many will turn away from the faith and will betray and hate each other, and many false prophets will appear and deceive many people. Because of the increase of wickedness, the love of most will grow cold, but the one who stands firm to the end will be saved." (Mathew 24:9-13).*
>
> *"How dreadful it will be in those days for pregnant women and nursing mothers! Pray that your flight will not take place in winter or on the Sabbath. For then there will be great distress, unequaled from the beginning of the world*

until now—and never to be equaled again". (Mathew 24:19-20).

"All this I have told you so that you will not fall away. They will put you out of the synagogue; in fact, the time is coming when anyone who kills you will think they are offering a service to God. They will do such things because they have not known the Father or me" (John 16:1-3)

"But before all this, they will seize you and persecute you. They will hand you over to synagogues and put you in prison, and you will be brought before kings and governors, and all on account of my name. And so you will bear testimony to me. But make up your mind not to worry beforehand about how you will defend yourselves. For I will give you words and wisdom that none of your adversaries will be able to resist or contradict. You will be betrayed even by parents, brothers and sisters, relatives and friends, and they will put some of you to death. Everyone will hate you because of me. But not a hair of your head will perish. Stand firm, and you will win life." (Luke 21:12-19).

Just like the disciples of old, so will be those that love Jesus. Hard times are ahead of us but as long as your faith is anchored in the Lord Jesus, there is no cause for alarm. He has promised to fight for those who love and trust Him. The question is how strong is your faith?

Even so, Lord Jesus, help us to stand firm to the end of time.

What the Bible Says About Snow

With so many inches of snow in Minnesota and other States, that made commuting either by air or road miserable, it's rather challenging to see any beauty in snow/winter. But looking at snow from inside the house is very beautiful indeed. Those who have at one time or the other committed sin, will find joy and happiness to know that if they repent, the good Lord will wipe away their sins to be as white as snow. This is indeed good news. Nothing makes me happy than to know that my sins will be wiped out to be as white as snow. Here is what the Bible says:

"Come now, let us settle the matter," says the LORD." Though your sins are like scarlet, they shall be as white as snow; though they are red as crimson, they shall be like wool. If you are willing and obedient, you will eat the good things of the land; but if you resist and rebel, you will be devoured by the sword." For the mouth of the LORD has spoken." (Isaiah 1:18-20).

And what about winter? A lot of people don't like winter for it's not only cold, but curtails many outside activities that we all enjoy. Life during winter is rather miserable as many find themselves hibernating. When talking about the persecution that His disciples will face, Jesus told all, more particularly pregnant women and those with babies, to pray that persecution does not happen either during the Sabbath day or winter season. Here is how He said it:" How dreadful it will be in those days for pregnant women and nursing mothers! Pray that your flight will not take place in winter or on the Sabbath. For then there will be great distress, unequaled from the beginning of the world until now—and never to be equaled again." (Mathew 24:19-21).

A Holiday Without Family Members

Each one of us has got family (spouse, siblings, children, parents), individuals that we love and want to be around them all the time. Some of the family members live closer to us; others are far away removed due to school, work and settling in another country. Sad to observe, some have passed on. I thank God for the holidays for they provide a golden opportunity for family members to gather, share stories/experiences, laugh and eat together. My wife and I are looking forward to the end of the year when we'll see, God willing, all our children who are now in schools in 4 different states. We just can't wait to see them. But today my mind is preoccupied with the decision of some to ignore family members? Ignore? Yes indeed. Here is how:

1. There are some spouses who for reasons best known to them, walked out and left the other spouse and children struggling on their own. Just think about the agony that such a deserted spouse and children feel. The emptiness and sense of betrayal are just too painful to think about. For whatever reason, they find themselves lost and alone in a world that can sure be lonely.
2. There are some who after marriage, decided to have nothing to do with their parents and siblings. Such hasn't seen any of their family members for years. Crying hasn't helped in any way.
3. There are others who left their native land for further studies. For years, they have ignored those that they left behind. No communication at all; no, not even calling, sending a card, or anything of that kind. Others decided to leave home and no one knows where they are. Just think about that.
4. There are many young people, mostly girls who voted in their boyfriends and voted out their parents and siblings.

Such are not only happy with their decision but also defend their decision with excitement.

And so as holidays come and go, there are many out there who spend such holidays crying and wondering whatever happened. Were their loved ones deceived, bewitched or what exactly happened? Hard to tell!

Well, even though those who walked away pretend that all is well, the truth of the matter is that we all at one time or the other have a deep desire to be connected to those that we have always loved. To them, my appeal is to do just what the prodigal son did:

"When he came to his senses, he said, 'How many of my father's hired servants have food to spare, and here I am starving to death! I will set out and go back to my father and say to him: Father, I have sinned against heaven and against you. I am no longer worthy to be called your son; make me like one of your hired servants.' So he got up and went to his father." (Luke 15:17-20).

Are you missing any of your family members? Pray that the good Lord will make a way for you to be connected or soften the hearts of those who are either deceived or bewitched. God can loosen all from their own imposed captivity

My prayers and thoughts are with all those who continue to mourn over their living loved ones. Pray and hope that you will be reunited someday.

It's Up To You

There are certain phrases/expressions that I find very interesting. One such is "it's up to you." Many are the times that I have needed someone's advice or opinion only to be told" It's up to you" I used to be annoyed with such kind of response until my children advised me" Get over with it", another interesting one.

But come to think about it, it is up to each one of us to decide on what we want to do and what not. Every single day, we are called upon to decide which route we want to take. One thing we should not forget, though, is that some decisions lead to untold pain and consequences. All in all, each one of us is of age to decide on which route/path that we want to travel in. Let us decide with great care avoiding those decisions that will in the long run affect us, those that we love and our God. As you decide, think of the following:

There is a way that seems right to a man, but in the end, it leads to death. (Proverbs 16:25)

"What benefit did you reap at that time from the things you are now ashamed of? Those things result in death!" (Romans 6:21)

"The way of a fool seems right to him, but a wise man listens to advise."(Proverbs 12:15)

1. The virtue of humility-I value humility so much that I am willing to buy it and not sell it. As I was growing up, I prayed to God to help me attain the highest education possible and yet become the meekest person in our time.

I’ve a long way of becoming like my heroes. Heroes? Yes, indeed!

2. To be like the prophet Moses, who was the meekest man on earth-Numbers 12:3
3. To be like the prophet Daniel who gave credit to the Lord of the universe-Daniel 2:26-28
4. To be like John the Baptist, who was willing to decrease for Jesus to increase -John 3:27-30)
5. To have the mind of Jesus-To have the mind of Jesus has been the dream of my life. To treat everybody like Jesus did and to be actively involved in spreading the good news is all that I want to do
6. I love/enjoy writing-A careful study of the gospels had a vey strong impact in my life. I was thrilled by the way Jesus took the ordinally and gave it a spiritual meaning. Over the years, I have taken the ordinary and gave it a spiritual lesson

Its my prayer that as you read these thoughts you will be able to discover the gem behind each one of them